Franchise: Freedom or Fantasy?

How to Know if a Franchise is Right for You After Your Corporate Career

Mitchell York
Professional Certified Coach

iUniverse, Inc.
New York   Bloomington

Franchise: Freedom or Fantasy?
How to Know if a Franchise is Right
for You After Your Corporate Career

iUniverse books may be ordered through booksellers or by contacting:

iUniverse
1663 Liberty Drive
Bloomington, IN 47403
www.iuniverse.com
1-800-Authors (1-800-288-4677)

ISBN: 978-1-4401-4849-1 (sc)
ISBN: 978-1-4401-4851-4 (dj)
ISBN: 978-1-4401-4850-7 (ebk)

Printed in the United States of America

iUniverse rev. date: 6/19/2009

773

For Nathan, with whom I fought the most,
and who fought alongside me the hardest,
as I transitioned from executive to entrepreneur

Contents

Chapter 1:
Getcha Smoothie Heah!

If you don't know where you are going, you might wind up someplace else.
—Yogi Berra

It's a smoldering late-August day in the Bronx in 2002. I am behind the counter of my smoothie kiosk at Yankee Stadium making frozen rum cocktails with my employee as fast as we can ladle smoothie mix, scoop ice, peel bananas, and blend it all in our Vita-Mix Drink Machine blenders.

Whirr!

Every fifteen seconds, we each pour two frosty concoctions onto shots of Bacardi at eight dollars a cup. The customer line is eight-feet deep, but we are moving them fast. It's mostly executives from Manhattan taking clients to the game. Sometimes a celebrity. We have served Spike Lee (piña colada, virgin), Marvin Hamlisch (strawberry banana with rum), Fred Willard (orange mango with rum), and countless others.

"Can I help the next customer, please?"

"Eight piña coladas!"

"Yes, sir. Sixty-four dollars."

We line up the drinks. The Suit peels a $100 bill from a wad of cash held together by a purple rubber band (the kind used on broccoli stalks) and slaps the money on the bar. He and his buddies take off with the drinks.

Between this concession stand and another we have on the stadium's upper level, we sell hundreds of drinks every game, the cash overflowing from of our fruit-stained aprons.

Yet, less than a year before, I could have been one of the suits on the other side of the bar. How did I wind up at the ballpark in a Hawaiian shirt slinging piña coladas?

Here is the short answer: after buying a smoothie franchise and attending a weekend of training with the company, I started dialing for venues from which to operate. My first call was to the Yankees. I talked their concession company into allowing me to set up my concession at the stadium. Within a few weeks of the launch of my business, I was operating in the best location (Gate 4, right by the main turnstiles) in the nation's most fabled baseball stadium and selling to the richest customers in the world. Even with the greedy house taking 50 percent of the revenue, we made out like bandits.

But how I got into business at Yankee Stadium is not the point of this particular story. If you spent time at the old Yankee Stadium, you would inevitably run into people you knew. I was just a few weeks into my business and hadn't had a chance to tell all of my friends from my corporate past what I was doing. One night I saw Scott, a former colleague who had worked closely with me at several companies. He was about eighth in the customer line. I saw him first and a moment later, he saw me. Initially, it didn't register with him. Then suddenly, when he was about sixth in line, his eyes got very wide, his jaw unhinged, and he said my name, almost to himself, as a question, although I could not hear him over the din and the booming voice of Manny, the six-foot-five concessionaire standing on a milk crate a few feet away bellowing, *"Proooogrammmmm! Getcha program heahhhhh!"*

"Mitch?"

Yes, Scott, it's Mitch. The guy who not long ago was president of an e-mail marketing company that had just gone public. The guy who had been senior vice president of the leading technology magazine publishing company in New York. The guy who had been president of LendingTree, Inc., in its start-up days.

I saw Scott's lips form the words, "What happened?"

Scott knew that I was laid off from my job as a senior vice president at Ziff Davis Media after 9/11 and thought that now I was hustling drinks in a Hawaiian shirt. Well, he was right! But that wasn't the whole story.

Baby Boomer/Corporate Refugee

Born in 1957, along with two million other Americans, I am a Baby Boomer. Neither of my parents went to college. My dad owned a deli in Manhattan where he worked six and sometimes seven days a week. My mom worked alongside him most of those days. We lived in an apartment in Queens, and because of their incredible hard work and frugal habits, my brother and I had everything we ever needed and wanted when we were growing up.

My parents sent my brother and me to one of the best private colleges in the country (Northwestern University) without any financial aid, and then I followed the path that was preset for me: to be a corporate executive. To work with my mind, not my body. To wear a suit and tie, not a beef-blood stained apron like my dad.

I raced through college, going to school for two summers so I could graduate in three years instead of four. Within a week of leaving bucolic Evanston, Illinois, (and a gorgeous girlfriend eight years older than me—was I nuts?) and moving back to my parents' apartment in Queens, I obtained my first job as an editorial assistant at a publishing house in New York. In another four weeks, I had my first apartment in the city, a five-floor walk-up on Eighty-first Street and First Avenue. The rent was $250 a month—half my take-home pay—but it was great to be on my own and on my way up in life.

From there it was mostly an up-the-ladder climb through companies and jobs. In 1981, I landed at a fast-growing business newspaper company called CMP Media, Inc. I started as a reporter for a construction-industry tabloid, and within three years, I was editor-in-chief of a start-up publication covering the travel industry. We quickly became market leaders. I traveled all over the country and the world solidifying our position with readers and advertisers.

Around 1984, I remember my boss asking me how much money I wanted to earn within five years. At the time, I was making about $50,000 a year. Trying to keep a straight face, I said $150,000, though I had no idea what I would do with that kind of money. I was a little bit off in my projection. By the end of the eighties, I was making more than $300,000 a year as a magazine publisher, and when I left the company in 1998, I was making more than $500,000 a year.

I was also burned out, depressed, and emotionally distant from my family. I was chasing something, but I didn't know what or why.

I hit a ceiling at CMP Media. The company went public, it became a lot more formal and political, and I was not playing the game well. So in 1998, I left to become president of LendingTree, which is now a household name but was then a fledgling start-up company. I was not at my best when I took on this incredible challenge, commuting between New York and Charlotte, North Carolina. While I accomplished many things that helped put the company on a successful track leading to its initial public stock offering and future success, I could not keep up the pace. I left after about a year and took a succession of senior management jobs with similar results. Something was wrong, but I didn't know exactly what.

The Day that Changed Everything

On September 11, 2001, I was in Atlanta at a trade show with about twenty people from Ziff Davis. A few minutes before 9:00 AM, I was getting ready to head to the convention center when my phone rang and one of my salespeople told me to turn on the TV.

Later that day, with the airports closed for at least the next few days, I secured a charter bus that would drive our group back to New York. We drove sixteen hours straight, crossing the Throgs Neck Bridge from the Bronx in the early morning of September 13. Looking west, we could see haze where the towers once stood.

Two months later, amid the immediate economic downturn triggered by the attacks, Ziff Davis eliminated the magazine publishing group I led. Along with several hundred people, I had lost my job. I pulled my résumé together and started having meetings with business magazine publishers and recruiters.

But my heart wasn't in it. I couldn't imagine taking yet another corporate job. In the months of my layoff, I had time to reflect on how little I really cared about the work I was doing. I valued the relationships with the people I worked with, but the products I sold were meaningless to me. I decided I needed to get as far away from corporate America as I could.

I was reading *The Wall Street Journal* one day and an article on franchising caught my eye. I had already been thinking about being in business for myself. After all, thanks to my parents, I had entrepreneurship in my genes. The next day, I picked up the *New York Times* and read an article about a new industry: executive coaching. It occurred to me that in all my corporate jobs, I was happiest and at my best when advising, mentoring, and cheering on others.

Reading those two articles within a day of each other led me to decide that there would be no more corporate jungle for me. I would do something by myself, for myself.

In early 2002, I started two businesses: a smoothie/coffee franchise and an executive coaching practice, helping other people—mostly fellow baby boomers—figure out how to disentangle themselves from the corporate world and move into a business that they could call their own.

Today, my two ventures are very successful and growing every year. However, looking back on the launch of these businesses, I discovered something about myself. I did not start my ventures from a defining vision. In retrospect, I was running away from corporate America, not running toward a new and better way of life. Because I wasn't sure of my business (or life) goals, I bumped into walls, got sidetracked often, and lived in perpetual doubt and fear, which lasted until my first coach—a wonderful guy from Maine named Doug Malcolm—helped me create a vision and a plan. He guided me as I shored up the holes in my personal foundation so I had the strength to move forward.

This book is an outgrowth of my entrepreneurial experience and my coaching of executives and start-up business owners. For years, I wondered what the connection was between the two paths I had chosen: franchise business owner and executive coach. While the connection makes perfect sense now, when I first started, I saw coaching as a hedge against the risks of my franchised business. If one didn't work out, the other one would.

Now it is clear to me that the two are intertwined and interdependent. As a coach/entrepreneur—a "player/coach" you might call it—I wake up every day with the same concerns, challenges, and motivations as my entrepreneur clients.

It has been nearly eight years since I cashed my last corporate paycheck. A few times along the way, I thought about chucking all this entrepreneur stuff and "getting back on the train," but I ripped up the tracks behind me long ago. The 6:32 to Penn Station does not pass my way anymore.

I consider myself successful and have a bright future because of the business and life strategy I have developed and implemented. I have no ax to grind; this is not going to be a sour-grapes rant against franchising from a disgruntled owner. My perspective is based on great success in franchising, a long career in corporate America, and years of experience as a trained and certified professional coach.

My story could save you or someone you know hundreds of thousands of dollars if you, or they, are thinking of buying a franchise or starting a small business.

Danger Ahead

We are in the midst of a worldwide economic shift. Thousands of people are losing their jobs every day. Many have experienced successful business careers, but now their employers are dumping them. Those who have lost their jobs may be shell-shocked, but many will have a relatively soft landing: a corporate buyout, an early retirement package, a pension. Having a bundle of cash to cushion the shock is certainly better than wondering how you are going to cover next month's mortgage payment. But that cash can do some real damage to you depending on your state of mind.

A blog post[1] by The Franchise King (a broker paid by franchisors when someone he attracts buys a franchise) illustrates my point about how a laid-off, emotionally fragile executive might be susceptible to a good sales pitch:

> *Microsoft is getting into the downsizing game, and in a huge way. When Microsoft fires 5,000 of its workers, all of us need to take notice.... Do you realize that 5,000 families have been impacted? This is the real story. I remember the 3–4 times when it happened to my dad. I remember the look on his face, each and every time it happened. It was*

---

1   The Franchise King Blog: "Job Losses Increasing; Is It Time To Be Your Own Boss?" January 23, 2009. http://tinyurl.com/ca5byv

> *a mixture of anger, sadness, and worry. As kids, (3 of us little munchkins) it was quite scary. Now, there are 5,000 families feeling what our little nuclear family felt. They are feeling it today. The question one needs to ask themselves is this: "How many more times will I have to feel this way before I get the courage to start owning what I do?"*

The Franchise King's line of reasoning plays on the emotions of potential entrepreneurs. It is very appealing to say to oneself, "This time I'm gonna stick it to the man, and be my own boss!" The king will probably profit handsomely selling franchises to families on the rebound. As will the franchisors he represents. If only "courage" were enough of a reason to start your own business. It is not.

Courageous or not, the armies of potential franchisees are on the march. In an insightful article on MSNBC.com, franchise consultant Mark Siebert notes, "Every 0.1 percent increase in the unemployment rate adds another 150,000 prospective franchise buyers to the marketplace."[2] Add to those the folks who are going to jump before they are pushed—Siebert calls them the "near layoffs"—and the pool grows larger still. Therefore, many workless people are sloshing around looking for something to do. Franchisors and franchise brokers are salivating!

But it gets better.

Many folks have already sold out of the stock market and are sitting on cash earning a low rate of interest in a money market account. These people are looking for ways to put their savings to work. While there may be fewer people willing to plunk down a million bucks for a Dunkin' Donuts franchise, those same people may fork over $500,000 or even as little as $50,000 for something else, and there are plenty of franchises available.

Siebert has a consulting firm that helps companies franchise their businesses, so he has a particular point of view supporting franchising. I don't support or criticize franchising. I am neutral. As a franchisee and a business coach, I know the pluses and minuses of owning a franchised business and the dangers faced by people going into a franchise for the wrong reasons. Still, I think Siebert's argument is valuable for

---

2   "A Bad Economy May Benefit Franchises," Entrepreneur.com, November 20, 2008. http://tinyurl.com/5ryydc

those who want to understand the economics at work in franchise sales. There was never a better time for buyers to beware than now.

Just look at the business results of companies like FranChoice, one of the biggest franchise brokers in the country. According to the *Minneapolis Star-Tribune*, FranChoice had two times the number of inquiries from prospective franchise owners in the last three months of 2008 compared with a year earlier—a direct reflection of massive displacement in the national work force. FranChoice's CEO says the company anticipates a "giant growth year" ahead. Millions of dollars are set to flow from workers' bank accounts, IRAs, and 401(k)s, and loans through mortgage brokers into the hands of franchisors. Many people will take the money they get from a corporate buyout or severance and buy themselves a job.

Living the Dream

A *Detroit News* article[3] tells the story of a Ford Motor employee who took a buyout, saw a Little Caesars Pizza commercial on TV, and bought a franchise. The president of Little Caesars is quoted in the article as saying that franchising is "a way [for people] to take their nest egg and invest it in something they can control … The more you put in, the more you get out."

This is an example of an overly simplistic sound bite that gets some people into deep trouble. The idea that you should take your nest egg and give it to Little Caesars and then gain "control," is something I cannot quite follow. In my view, the franchisor is the one with the control. They have control over the products you sell, the way you sell, and they control your cash register from which they withdraw their royalties.

The customers buying pizza have control: they can buy from you or Famous Ray's Pizza or Domino's, or get a burger. The employees making the pizza have control: they can show up for work or not, and if they do, they may show up physically but not mentally.

The owner does not have so much control. The owner has to cough up as much as $500,000 to open a Little Caesars store. The company, on its Web site, encourages people with as little as $50,000 in liq-

---

3   *Detroit News*, October 10, 2008. "Workers open franchises with buyouts" by Jaclyn Trop. http://tinyurl.com/cyrnat

uid assets and a net worth as low as $150,000 to apply![4] This means some people who are a few steps away from being financially wiped out could apply and possibly be awarded a franchise. They may have to go into debt up to their eyeballs to live the pizza dream, but hey, they're courageous! Many, no doubt, bought the dream—and some surely are succeeding. Others probably wound up in a cheesy nightmare.

The bottom line is don't fall in love with the idea of business ownership. It is no easier than working for "the man" in a corporate job. Actually, it is much, much harder.

The Voice in Your Ear

Some people will read this book and decide to move forward with franchising or some other type of business opportunity. They'll buy a business that someone else is desperate to get rid of—perhaps a local coffee house or a muffler shop. Or they will cruise the Web's many franchise sites and start talking to consultants who will help them find a franchise. They will perceive strength in numbers. There are more than three thousand franchise firms with over one million locations nationwide, adding up to a $2.3 trillion industry, according to the International Franchise Association. The number of franchise businesses grew by 18 percent from 2001 to 2005, compared with 15 percent growth of independent businesses, according to a 2008 study commissioned by the IFA.

"If all those other people can start a franchised business, why not me?" will be a common thought running through millions of minds in the coming years.

Once these people are in the franchise evaluation process, they will be exposed to subtle, but very intense, sales techniques that will pressure them to make a decision quickly, usually within four to six weeks. They'll be told all the caveats by the franchisor—it's their business and they are responsible for its success or failure. Their final phone call with the franchisor before awarded a franchise may be recorded. They'll be asked many legal disclaimer questions, and they will say, clear as a bell, that they understand the success of their business is up to them, not the franchisor. They will sign a franchise agreement that gives nearly all legal rights and protections to the franchisor. And finally, they will

---

4   http://tinyurl.com/dhl7nl

feel the endorphins rush as they write a huge check—possibly the biggest of their lives, similar in size to buying a house or funding a college education—as a down payment on their new life as an entrepreneur.

For many, buying a franchise after a bad work experience is a little bit like a rebound romance. You've been unexpectedly jilted. Your confidence is shaken. To distract yourself, you start Googling and clicking, and before you know it, you're a franchisee. You're still hurting from what happened in your job as you embark on something that will test your limits as nothing has before. You are not running toward something as much as running away from something—the pain of losing what you had before. And it's just a matter of time before you can't run fast enough or far enough to get away from yourself.

This book is for people who may be caught up in the economic turmoil of our day; for those who have reached a point in their corporate careers where they've achieved success, have a lot to show for it, and just want out of the rat race. And it's for those who seek coaching through the early stages of franchised and small business so they can create the success they deserve. After you read this, should you take the plunge into franchising or other business ownership after corporate life, you will be running toward a very specific, unique vision of what you want for yourself and your family. I wish you fulfillment and success.

Chapter 2:
On the Run

Don't look back. Something might be gaining on you.

—Satchel Paige

Have you read the latest issue of the *New England Medical Gazette*? If you're an executive who is thinking of going entrepreneur, you need to check it out. Turns out there is a newly discovered condition affecting entrepreneurs called ABF. Unlike restless legs syndrome and erectile dysfunction, there's no drug to treat it yet, so you will have to manage this condition without a prescription.

Oh, ABF stands for *Accumulated Boss Fatigue*. I first noticed I was developing ABF about five years before I left corporate America. I am glad to be able to share the details of my condition so that others may find relief.

Stage One, Independence Day. How do you know you may have ABF? For me, it happened after years of dutiful service to various employers. I found myself forgetting that I had a boss. I was routinely making decisions and taking actions that were contrary to what the boss asked me to do. Even worse, I often didn't bother letting the boss know I had absolutely no intention of following through on the ridiculous stuff she had asked of me. This early onset stage is called RIS—*Raging Independence Syndrome*. It's curable at this stage if you get back in line, apologize, maybe take some time off to clear your head, and remember that in most companies, the nail that stands out is hammered down. If that doesn't work, you're on your way to Stage Two.

Stage Two, Craving the Movie, Office Space. When the film came out in 1999, I felt I was watching my autobiography. My job may have been bigger and less cubicle-bound than the characters in the movie had, but I could relate. I must have watched the film a dozen times that year. And whenever I had a meeting with my boss, I saw the face of Lumbergh in my mind and heard "*Yeahhhhhh. Thannnkssss.*" That's stage two, and from there, you're pretty much a goner.

Stage Three, Anything but this Job. You know you've reached doneness when you are poked with a fork and your juices run clear; when any other type of work (like, for instance, being a concessionaire at Yankee Stadium) appeals to you more than what you are currently doing, and any face would be a refreshing change from your Lumberghian boss's. There's a danger here, though. When you decide to go it alone in business, make sure you're doing it for the right reasons, at the right time, and with the right support—not just to run away from your battle with ABF.

Say Hi To Rena

To illustrate this point, I'd like you to meet Rena. Rena's not real. I invented her. She's a composite of many mid-life baby boomers, and I think you'll find her quite lifelike. She may resemble people you know—maybe you'll even see some of yourself reflected in her.

Rena's forty-five years old. She has been working in Information Technology for most of her career and has been very successful. She's a senior project manager for a consulting company, working on implementations of complex software for companies around the globe. She travels about 60 percent of the time. She used to love business travel: three trips a year to Europe, another two to Asia, and about twenty domestic trips in between. For long-haul flights, she used to fly business class before the economic downturn, but now she has to travel economy and upgrade with her frequent-flier points when seating space is available. The domestic flights from Boston where she lives to cities like Dallas, Minneapolis, Tampa, and Oklahoma City, have made her an airport expert and an all-too-frequent customer of Chili's.

Rena and her husband Keith have three children, ages fourteen, eighteen, and nineteen. The oldest one has just started college and tuition is high. Rena's base salary is $175,000 a year, and her husband's high school teacher salary is $65,000 a year. They don't qualify for federal financial aid, so they are paying retail for college. She and her husband have a house worth $700,000 (with a mortgage of $500,000 because of a home-equity loan they took out to remodel a few years ago). They have about $300,000 in their 401(k)s, down 43 percent from a year earlier, and about another $200,000 in marketable securities. They have saved about $75,000 in custodial 529 accounts for each of their children's college educations (down only 23 percent from a year earlier because of their conservative investment choices for those funds). They owe $35,000 on a low-interest credit card loan, which they used to buy a new Ford Edge for Rena. (Keith drives a 1998 Subaru Outback with 120,000 miles.) They pay about $5,500 a year for car insurance (including more than $2,700 for their eighteen-year-old son). They put about 5 percent of their net take home pay into savings. They also put the maximum allowed into their 401(k) retirement plans. They consider themselves middle class.

Rena is very tired. She works twelve hours a day and doesn't feel the same energy, motivation, or excitement she did years ago. For the past month or two—she can't remember exactly—she's been thinking about getting out of technology and corporate life completely. She fantasizes about working for herself on her own terms. Not having to travel. No boss to manage. No more Chili's restaurant meals. More time at home with her family.

One night, she and Keith were in bed, he grading senior history papers and she checking e-mail on her notebook. After surfing recipes for tonight's leftover chicken, she Googled "business opportunities in Boston," and 1,520,000 results showed up 0.29 seconds later. Several on the first page were for franchises. She figured, "What the heck," and before turning out the lights for the night, she clicked on an ad and filled out a form for more information.

The next day at work, Rena received a phone call from a franchise consultant. While she's usually not the type to take calls from people she doesn't know, she closed her office door and had a long chat with Kathleen, a franchise consultant and broker based in Atlanta. Kathleen was really great to talk to. Rena enjoyed her southern accent and friendliness. Kathleen was very empathetic. About the same age as Rena, Kathleen was working from her home office after a long career in corporate sales for Dell Computer. Kathleen and Rena talked for about forty-five minutes. Encouraged by Kathleen, Rena opened up about her frustrations at work and her desire to make a big career change in her life. With a checklist in her hand, Kathleen asked many questions about the type of life and business Rena might like, and she followed up two days later with a long e-mail reconfirming what Rena had told her. Attached to the e-mail was a document with details about four franchises for Rena to consider.

Fast-forward two weeks. Two of the four franchises Kathleen presented to her intrigued Rena. She initiated discussions with the two franchisors, received and reviewed their federally mandated Franchise Disclosure Documents, and started due diligence research. After another week, Rena ruled out one of the franchises and continued investigation of the other.

She dived into the homework the franchisor had assigned: creating spreadsheet models, interviewing franchisees selected for her by the franchisor, and writing essays on why she would be a good franchisee. She enjoyed the franchise investigation process; her franchisor was in command choreographing her every move. She liked being given all these tasks and ticking them off her list. She felt productive and engaged—similar to how she felt when she first started at her current job.

Her husband was supportive, though not overly enthusiastic. Keith's feeling was that if Rena wanted to start a business, she should go for it. Personally, he was happy as a reasonably well paid and secure civil servant with five more years to go before retiring with a nice pension and the prospect of starting a second career.

During the next two weeks, Rena had six more conversations with Kathleen, articulating her concerns and fears. Kathleen was attentive and listened well, encouraging Rena to take control of her life—whether or not she opted for a franchise. Rena really appreciated the support of another woman of Kathleen's experience.

Rena had four more conversations with the franchisor during the same period. They, too, were encouraging. They told her she would go through many emotions in the process of deciding what to do, but that they believed she'd be a great business owner based on her experience and profile, and that fear was a normal part of the process.

Then, Rena jumped.

She resigned from her job and bought a shop-at-home interior decorating franchise. She spent $45,000 on the franchisee fee and committed to investing another $150,000 in the coming ninety days on training, a customized van, fabric samples, equipment, inventory, labor, insurance, an advertising fund and more. She financed the expenses by liquidating most of her and her husband's stocks, taking a big loss from where they were a year ago. After all, she thought the market could keep going down, and she asked herself is there any better use of money than investing in yourself? That's what Kathleen told her about a month ago, which was the last time Kathleen had checked in after Rena bought the franchise. Rena missed Kathleen's calls.

She packed her bags for Portland, Oregon, for training with her new franchise, eager to read on the plane her copies of *The E-Myth* and *The Millionaire Next Door*, sent to her by the franchisor as part of the welcome package. Was that knot in her stomach airplane turbulence or something more? She closed her eyes and slept.

Are You a Rena?

Thousands of Rena's sign up for franchises every day. I worry about Rena and here's why. She approached franchising and business ownership on something of a whim. Business ownership was not a long-time goal of hers. Once she started looking into it though, it became more and more appealing. It was a way out of a dreary job without having to go through the résumé writing, the letter writing, the networking, the interviewing, and the on boarding of a new job. She was running away from her job, and it felt very good to her.

Rena chose to start a business even though she had never run a company before buying her franchise. No one in her family had ever run a business either, so there were no entrepreneurial role models for her to emulate. Both her parents were teachers. In college, she majored in computer science and was something of a wallflower—a follower not a leader. She never held a sales position, and in fact, disliked the idea of selling. Her franchisor administered a personality profile test as part of her franchise investigation and the results said she'd be good at following a system. (Well, of course she would, she majored in computer science!)

Does this sound like someone who'd be a natural in a franchise, or indeed, any business of her own? Yet, every year, tens of thousands of people with backgrounds just like Rena's go into franchised businesses, where there is a premium on traits like problem solving, management ability, leadership, sales skill, marketing, budgeting, and finance. Some franchise experts will say Rena's background is just fine. As long as the franchise business model is sound, Rena can hire the people she needs to fill in her skill gaps and then follow the instructions given in training, and *voila*, profits are likely to follow.

But franchising is not a guarantee of success. It's an opportunity for success for some, and a truckload of rope with which others can hang themselves. Franchising is most certainly not something people should be doing out of boredom or frustration. Quite the opposite. If you want to start a business, franchised or not, you should feel on top of your game, invincible, and never better. You should have lots of money saved, be brimming with confidence, have unflagging family support, and lots of relevant experience. You should be running toward what you see as a fantastic opportunity with so much momentum that not all the obstacles in the world can stop you.

If you are about to sign on the dotted line for a franchise and aren't feeling like that, ***Put. The. Pen. Down. Now.***

The "Running Away vs. Running Toward" Quiz

How do you know if you are running toward a vision of success or running away from problems you don't want to face? Circle your answer to these questions to find out.

1. I have been thinking seriously about starting my own business for a year or more.	T	F
2. I have savings that will last my family and me at least five years if the worst-case scenario occurs.	T	F
3. I feel highly confident in myself and believe I can succeed at anything I set my mind to.	T	F
4. I am willing and able to work harder than at any other time in my life.	T	F
5. I feel rested, healthy, and have had a medical checkup in the past six months. I have no disease or condition that I know of that may slow me down.	T	F

6. My spouse/partner is 100 percent supportive of my buying a franchise and is ready to help in any way I need.	T	F
7. There is not a single job in the world I can see myself doing now. I have to start a business.	T	F
8. I am a self-starter and do not need anyone to tell me what to do next or how to prioritize my workload.	T	F

If you circled True to every one (not just some) of the statements above, you may be ready to buy a franchise. If you circled False to one or more, stop and think. You need more time. This may not be the right opportunity for you or the right time. There is no hurry, despite the deadlines imposed on you by your franchise broker, your prospective franchisor, or yourself.

The quiz above is a good self-barometer of where you stand in the soul-searching you may need to do about entrepreneurship. Here's a little more information to help you.

Give it a Year

One way to know you are running toward a vision of business ownership is when the drive to do so has been on your mind for at least a year.

Why a year?

You're thinking, "A year? Is he nuts? So much can happen in a year. I might be on to something else by then."

Exactly!

We all go through ups and downs throughout a year's time. We go through seasonal cycles, mood swings, issues with our jobs that may last a month or two or longer. We have issues with our spouses and partners, most of which come and go.

If an idea or plan sits with you through four seasons and is still front and center, you have a basis to move forward. My coach, Leah Grant, likes to say there's a big difference between taking a risk and putting yourself at risk. Time to reflect is an instrumental part of making sure you're taking only healthy risks.

Feel the Fear and have a Contingency Plan

If you have self-doubts or question your ability to succeed in business, listen to your inner voice. I don't believe the idea espoused in many business books that one should "feel the fear, but do it anyway." I believe in listening to your fears and making a judgment about whether your fears are real or imagined. Yes, sometimes we let negativity and what self-help guru Tony Robbins calls "limiting beliefs," get in the way of what we can achieve. But at other times, fear is what keeps us alive. So go ahead, be afraid. *Be very afraid.* Then examine your fears and decide whether you can fully get over them and then move ahead. Then, and only then, should you proceed into entrepreneurship.

Assessing Your Fears Exercise

Here's a self-reflection exercise you can use to understand your fears about starting a business. Answer these questions after thinking about them for at least thirty minutes.

1. What is the worst that could happen if I fail in my business?

_____

_____

_____

_____

2. What is the probability that the worst will happen? _____%

3. How would failure in business affect my family members and my relationships?

_____

_____

_____

4. What are my alternatives to starting a business?

_____

_____

_____

5. What is the probability that I will be successful through one of those alternatives? _____%

6. Am I likely to be more or less successful with one of the alternatives to starting my own business? Why?

_____

_____

_____

This is the time and place where you have the freedom to ask and answer the big questions. After you have written the checks, signed the lease, and bought the inventory, the train has already left the station. So really think about the scenarios.

What is the worst that could happen if you fail? For some people, the worst is they'll pick up the pieces and move on, even if they have to repay debts for years. Others may envision their family falling apart and being homeless.

Some people will envision four or five solutions to their current dissatisfaction other than starting a business, and wonder why they haven't seriously considered those alternatives. One reason might be that they are harder, in the short run, than just throwing money at the problem (if you have money to throw). But what if, after reflection, you see that the problem can be corrected and you can have a satisfying new career that does not involve the risk and sacrifice of business ownership. Shouldn't you give that serious consideration?

Be Fired Up and Ready to Go 24/7

Are you ready to work like a maniac? Because as a franchisee, you will, especially in the first few years of your business. The only people who do not work like fiends for the first several years are those who are on their way to failure. Got a lazy streak? Like to sleep late? Committed to taking long family vacations? Like to read the Sunday newspapers? Go do all that. Just don't be in your own business.

Think I'm exaggerating? Here are some of the daily activities you might do as a brand new business owner and for your first two years or more in business, which of course will vary depending on the type of business:

- Interviewing, hiring, training, and firing employees

- Preparing for a "Secret Shopper" visit from your franchisor
- Fixing the Point-of-Sale system
- Calculating royalty payments
- Planning cash flow to meet expenses
- Dealing with bank overdrafts
- Designing a marketing brochure, ad campaign, coupon
- Talking to your accountant, banker, insurance representative, attorney, plumber, chamber of commerce, auto mechanic, carpenter, union shop steward, etc.
- Greeting customers and figuring out how to get more business from them
- Checking up on competition
- Opening, closing, filling in for a sick employee, dealing with a difficult customer
- Handling worker's compensation
- Reordering supplies

I'm sure you can add a few dozen other items to the potential daily list of activities. You will be very busy.

Be Healthy as a Horse

If you are serious about buying a franchise and are nearing the finish line, get a complete physical. A few years ago, a close friend of mine who was in business for himself was unexpectedly sidetracked for months with a major illness. Fortunately, by that time he had other people to help him stay in business. But even with the help, he was thrown off his game for about six months. He considered getting out of his business. He started casting around to see what the job market was like, and had someone offered him a halfway decent job, he would have taken it. He's glad no one did. If he had become ill in his first year in business, there might not have been a second year. I have seen more people go out of franchised businesses due to health reasons than any other cause—even cash flow.

You can't foresee everything when it comes to health, but do all you can to stay healthy. At the very least, get a complete physical and get all of the recommended preventative tests for someone your age. Plan for what happens if you do become injured or sick. If you have no one to back you up in your business that should give you great pause. Do anything preventative you can think of including visiting your dentist and your eye doctor. Speak to a health insurance consultant. Plan, plan, plan, because once you buy into your business and the train is moving, stopping is a very costly option.

It is also a good idea to be in as good physical condition as possible. If you need to lose fifteen pounds, I recommend you do it before you buy a franchise. Why? Well, there are the obvious benefits to being in shape. But no matter what kind of business you might enter, if you're going to be the boss, you will probably be more physically active than when you worked for a large company. In the good old days of corporate employment, did someone deliver your mail? Your coffee? Fix your computer? Did a car service pick you up to go to the airport? Did you spend a lot of time sitting in meetings? When you own a business, you will be doing many things for yourself that someone else may have done, plus all of the other responsibilities that go along with owning a small business. Most franchises are not "sit behind a desk" businesses. There are pet grooming businesses, sandwich shops, muffler repair, hardware stores, real estate firms, and thousands more. So lighten up. Literally.

One more thing: if you don't have the discipline to get in shape (and that includes quitting smoking, losing weight, getting your blood pressure under control, and other health to-do's), it's a real question as to whether you have the discipline to be in your own business. No one will be telling you what to do or when to do it, so if you don't take the initiative as the owner, the business will suffer and possibly even fail. (I think they call my little speech here "tough love.")

You and the Joneses

If you have a spouse or a partner, is that person fully on board with your becoming an entrepreneur? I have seen marriages and relationships crumble in a dramatically short time because of the strains of a start-up business, usually tied to not having enough cash to weather the first few years. I knew a guy whose wife was gung ho at the beginning and helped him out all the time. But she quickly grew weary of the business and long hours, especially when she had to make sacrifices in their lifestyle—no more vacations, no more dinners out. Wait a second, she didn't sign up for that! It was the end of their marriage and it unwound in a hurry. She divorced him, they sold their house, and he moved out of state to get work. He rarely sees his children. A sad picture, indeed.

But it's not only about money: the lifestyle of a franchisee is very different from just about any other job. Many new franchisees had careers that gave them a certain level of respectability in their communities. In a franchise, that often goes out the window.

Like me, you may find yourself wearing a Hawaiian shirt and a goofy baseball cap and getting your hands sticky. You may be ready for that, but is your spouse or partner ready? Ideas about status and professions can change quickly. Remember how schoolteachers were thought to be underachievers. ("Those who can't, teach.") Well, now teachers are looking pretty darn smart—a reliable paycheck and an outstanding pension after thirty years of service. So perceptions can change. But if you live in Shaker Heights, Ohio, or Garden City, New York, or Palm Beach, Florida, and one day your Lexus is replaced in the driveway by a van with a decal on the side, your friendly neighbors might be anything but friendly from then on.

Discouraged Yet?

If I've given you pause with my litany of what can go wrong, good! For the small price of this book, you've saved tens or hundreds of thousands of dollars. But my guess is that you aren't discouraged. You just want to give yourself the best chance for success. In the next chapters, you'll see how many franchise and other business owners achieved success through habits and practices you can emulate.

Chapter 3:
Step Back for Self-Reflection

One does not discover new lands without consenting to lose sight of the shore for a very long time.

—Andre Gide

When you start investigating a franchise through either a franchise broker or a franchisor directly, you may become focused on which franchise is right for you. That's an important question, but not as important as knowing whether any franchise is right for you.

Remember, your franchise broker wants you to buy a franchise, and it really doesn't matter to her which one. Sure, she will offer you the ones she feels are best for you, but don't expect her to walk away from a 20 percent commission—perhaps as much as $10,000 or $20,000—just because she thinks you might not make a great business owner.

Franchise brokers are just like real estate brokers. They want you to buy a house—any house. And once you do, you may never see or hear from them again. Does this make franchise brokers bad people? No, of course not. One of my good friends is a franchise broker and he's a terrific, ethical guy. Let's assume they are all wonderful, ethical human beings. That doesn't change the fact that they are there for one purpose only: to facilitate the buying and selling of franchises.

Kendra Kerr, a franchise broker for The Entrepreneur's Source, told me this: "Most people can get into franchising easily, regardless of their characteristics. I conduct an assessment to understand their communication [and] leadership style. The assessment is a terrific tool for cluing me in on the type of franchise that would be most appropriate for my client.

"As an example, someone who is highly compliant, very task oriented and [has] minimal people skills would be best suited for a franchise where people come to them. Extroverts who are goal-oriented would be best suited for a direct sales type of franchise. Both types of people need to be able to follow a process."

I have no doubt that Kendra's assessment tools help point people in the direction of an appropriate franchise. But I question whether characteristics such as "compliance" and "minimal people skills" are useful traits for any business owner, franchise or otherwise.

Think of a half dozen people you know who are successful in their own businesses. Is there one of them who got there by being "task oriented" with "minimal people skills"? Maybe you can come up with one. I know several dozen highly successful business owners personally and I can't come up with even one that fits that description.

Perhaps one could argue if you buy a franchise that has a great brand name—let's say Great Clips or Subway—that as long as you keep the place clean and the shelves stocked, you can be successful even if you don't like dealing with the public.

Owners set the tone. If they don't like dealing with the public, that attitude will show up in the people they hire. If they don't like dealing with their employees (part of the owner's "public") they will not hire the kinds of people who help an owner develop a loyal clientele.

Of course, hundreds of franchises limit their exposure to people, but I don't think there are any that eliminate it. And where there are people to deal with, there is the need for a wide range of skills that not everyone possesses in sufficient measure.

Compared with franchise brokers, franchisors will be more discriminating about whether you fit what they are looking for in a franchisee. But more often than not, money talks. If you have the money, you are likely to be accepted—especially now, with franchisors hurting economically and looking for franchise fees to keep their lights on and payrolls going.

The franchisor has little to lose. Yes, if you fail it's a black mark against them that has to be disclosed in the Franchise Disclosure Document. And the cost of dealing with a failed franchisee can be considerable. But for the franchisor, these risks are minimal. Most franchisees, when they go, go quietly. Franchise brokers and franchisors won't tell you what the true critical skills are for success. But I will. And I will do more than that. I will tell you how you can improve some of those skills if you're not strong enough now.

Two Self-Reflection Tests

Prior to discussing the critical success skills for franchise owners, now is the perfect time for some introspection. Earlier, I asked if you've been thinking about starting a business venture for at least a year. That's a good start. Here's a little more reassurance to test your desire.

If you want to know what you can do to be sure there's an entrepreneur (franchise or otherwise) locked inside you waiting to emerge and that you are ready to run toward your vision, and not away from other problems, take these two tests. I came across the basic idea for the following technique from the Five O'Clock Club, which is the nation's leading job and career-coaching company. (I am proud to be a member of their Coaching Guild, and I use their methodologies in my career coaching. You can learn more about them at www.fiveoclockclub.com.) Their technique is very adaptable to potential entrepreneurs.

Accomplishments Quiz

Answer the following question:

What are five things you have done in your life that are your most noteworthy accomplishments?

You can list professional accomplishments as well as personal ones, and you can go back as far as you want in your life—don't limit yourself to adulthood. Ideally, come up with a list of a lot more than five—up to twenty-five—then pare them down to five and list them here.

1._____

2._____

3._____

4._____

5._____

Reflecting on the accomplishments you listed, what characteristics, and traits of your personality enabled you to accomplish what you did?

Accomplishment	Traits
1	
2	
3	
4	
5	

Failures Quiz

Okay, next question. What are the five things you have done in your life that are your most noteworthy failures (business and/or personal)?

1._____
2._____
3._____
4._____
5._____

Reflecting on the failures and disappointments you listed, what characteristics and traits of your personality allowed these things to occur?

Failure/Disappointment	Traits

Spend an hour (or more, but not less) reflecting on these exercises and answer these questions.

1. What do your accomplishments reveal about you and your personality?

_____

_____

_____

2. What do your failures and disappointments reveal about you and your personality?

_____

_____

_____

3. What traits do you possess that would be important for success as an entrepreneur?

_____

_____

_____

4. What traits do you possess that could potentially cause you problems or failure as an entrepreneur?

_____

_____

_____

5. Do you see any gaps between what you believe are the critical success factors of business ownership and the traits you've demonstrated when at your best? What are you missing?

_____

_____

_____

Just a little self-reflection about how you have engaged success and failure in the past before starting a business can make it less—or more—scary, but either way, the questions are important to ask.

Self-reflection is the most important step in determining whether you are running toward or away from something in the process of deciding whether to become a business owner.

Unfortunately, too many people are caught up in the excitement and momentum of what they think entrepreneurship entails, and they don't properly assess their strengths and weaknesses, unique life situation, and alternatives.

Now, onto what I believe to be the critical skills for success in franchising. From the exercises above, you may already have a good idea of which ones you possess and which ones you need to work on.

Chapter 4:
The Critical Skills
You Need to Succeed

Success is simply a matter of luck. Ask any failure.

—Earl Wilson

Skill #1. High Risk Tolerance

No one knows for sure whether he or she will be successful as a franchise owner or in any other kind of business until he or she actually tries. That doesn't mean all people should try. Some should opt-out after a careful assessment of a number of factors. Risk tolerance is the primary one.

Everyone knows starting a business is risky. Most people also believe starting a franchised business is less risky than a non-franchised business. That's a debatable point for which no reliable data exist.

For some people, franchises are indeed less risky because you start with an established brand (maybe) and a proven operating system (you hope). But in reality, the extent to which a franchise mitigates risk depends on the potential franchisee's core skills and personality.

For others, a franchise is no less risky than other business types because other factors—like their inherent abilities and business instincts—outweigh any gain of perceived safety a franchise may offer.

Franchises can be more expensive to start than non-franchised businesses. If you want to start a cafe, all you need is a rented space, coffee grinders, espresso equipment, hot and cold running water, a menu

29

board, cups, and off you go. If you do the same with a franchised company, you have to use *their* menu board, *their* cups, *their* espresso machine, *their* awning, *their* uniforms, all "their" stuff sold to you at a significant markup, which potentially increases your start-up cost by a factor of two or more.

Add to that your franchise fee and you are deep in the hole before you sell your first half-caff, half-decaf skinny vanilla, extra foam latte.

So put aside the notion that franchises are automatically less risky and go back to the question: how do you feel about risk?

Do you like Las Vegas or Atlantic City? Do you place a friendly bet on ball games? Do you trade a lot in the stock market? (Are you a shortseller or options trader? Your risk profile just went way up!) Do you like activities some people would consider dangerous, like skydiving, driving a motorcycle, or mountain climbing? Did you see the film *Into the Wild* and identify with the main character? (If so, you're a born franchisee!) Do you go "all in" when you feel strongly about something, rather than diversify your risk?

The way you answer the above questions may give you a sense of how much risk you are comfortable with.

Business Owner as Riverboat Gambler

I have worked with and for many CEOs and business founders who were the high-stakes gambler types. The lessons their stories reveal can help you determine if you have the right stuff for franchise or any other type of entrepreneurship.

One of them was Doug Lebda, the CEO/founder of LendingTree, the mortgage service whose slogan, "When banks compete, you win," is now ubiquitous.

I was president of LendingTree in its early days. At one point in 1998, I remember we had enough cash in the bank to last three weeks. We were feverishly working to bring more investment into the company. I was losing sleep and starting to stare into the abyss, but Doug wasn't at all fazed. I remember saying to him, "You sure do enjoy living on the edge." To which he replied with a wry grin, "This isn't even close to the edge."

That was an amazing statement from a guy who had borrowed and mortgaged everything he had and taken millions more from investors to get his company going. Doug was a master at presenting a game face to investors, looking like a million bucks when he was asking for $10 million!

A few years later, Doug sold the company, which had gone public, to media mogul Barry Diller for about $750 million. Doug was an "all-in" entrepreneur. Recently, he invested $3.5 million of his own money to buy stock in the new company formed after Diller spun off Lending Tree and related acquisitions into a new entity. So Doug is starting all over again, a serial entrepreneur who loves a risky bet.

Another CEO I know is a supreme bluffer. Let's call him Bob the Bluffer. When negotiating with potential business partners and suppliers, he promises huge volumes of purchases in the future. The vendors on the other side of the table can't believe their good fortune and are dying to give Bob a discount on purchases they wouldn't give anyone else because they are convinced of the riches to come.

The big orders don't come, but by then Bob is negotiating with other vendors for the same big discounts. Risky? You bet. The bluffer strategy puts the company's reputation at risk and establishes a company culture that is less about honesty and forthrightness than expediency.

But guess what? Bob and his business are still alive while many other businesses in his category are dead. So while you may not like his tactics, you have to admire his resiliency.

The lesson here is there is no such thing as a risk-averse entrepreneur. If you do not believe that you can lose a fortune and then make it all back, that you can outplay anyone else's hand, and that you will be the last woman standing in a brawl, then you are not going to be a successful entrepreneur. That is true whether you start a franchise or non-franchise business.

If you believe a franchisor when they tell you that as a franchisee you will be in business "for yourself but not by yourself" (which they all say), and you interpret this to mean someone is sharing the risk with you, you are not going to be a successful entrepreneur.

If you believe you have the skills to be a franchise entrepreneur, but are not skillful enough to be the kind of entrepreneur who can do what Doug and Bob did, you are not going to be a successful entrepreneur.

I am not saying you have to be able to sell your franchise for $750 million like Doug did or wrangle semi-shady deals like Bob, but whether your business is going to be worth $750 million or $750,000 is not the point.

Creating value is what it's all about. If all you want to do is produce an owner's income of $75,000 a year (or some other figure), you are not an entrepreneur—you have merely bought yourself a job rather than found one elsewhere. Not that there's anything wrong with that, but let's call it what it is.

Here's another example of an entrepreneur who offers a great object lesson. Rosalind Resnick was CEO of a company called NetCreations, a pioneer in e-mail marketing in the mid-1990s. I was president and a board member. The smartest thing Rosalind did was never to take a penny from investors. She had a 49 percent partner who was the chief technology officer of the company. For about five years, she built up the company and it was carried by the strong Internet tide to the beach of success in 2000 with an initial public offering.

No sooner had the company gone public, than the bubble burst. The stock slid rapidly from above $50 to the low teens. Charmer that she was (with perfect French, *bien sûr!*), she convinced a French marketing company to buy NetCreations for $111 million in cash, about $13 a share. So what if the company's market value was once $700 million. Rosalind walked away with around $35 million in, as she loved to say, "Cold, hard cash!"

Rosalind succeeded for one reason—and it wasn't that the company's business was especially valuable or unique. She was a huge risk-taker and expert negotiator. Over expensive bottles of Bordeaux, she could take on some slick French executives in double-breasted suits and not blink.

She could also resist doing the easy thing, which would have been to take some of the money that was churning around from venture capital sources and spend it on nicer offices or a better software system.

At one point, I tried to convince Rosalind to spend more than a million dollars on a complete rebuild of the software that was the core of the business's operation. When the existing software hiccupped, which was often, millions of e-mails that were supposed to go out on behalf of our clients were delayed. However, she knew it would have made no sense to make that investment, and she was right: the company was sold a few months later.

Most mere mortals would have diluted their equity along the way and cashed out for a sure thing, but Rosalind did not. She bet big and won, even though the company eventually went away and no one missed it.

You don't have to have executive risk-taking experience to be a card-carrying risk taker. Take my friend Ron, for example. He's an attorney. About twenty years ago, he bought a seat on the Chicago Mercantile Exchange, but not because he intended to trade pork bellies. He just wanted an investment that might have a payoff down the road, and he was willing to pony up $50,000—a lot of money to spend for a young lawyer with toddlers running around.

His risky investment paid off. He sold his seat for more than a million dollars last year. To be a successful franchise entrepreneur, you have to possess core skills related to risk-tolerance. Don't let yourself be fooled that because you are considering a franchise you need to be any less entrepreneurial than Doug or Bob or Rosalind or Ron. Answer these questions and see how you do.

The Franchise Entrepreneur Risk-O-Meter Test

Money is Like Doritos. I am prepared to lose 100 percent of my franchise investment if I cannot make my business successful.	T	F
Don't Blame the Franchisor. The franchisor has very little or nothing to do with whether or not I will be successful.	T	F
The Thrill of Defeat. I have experienced one or more big defeats in the past and it does not deter me.	T	F
I Am My Own Best Stock. If I had $500,000 of available capital, I would rather buy a franchise or start a business than invest in a financial instrument that would guarantee me a competitive return forever.	T	F

The quiz above gives you some solid insight into the characteristics of entrepreneurs. If you answered True to all these statements, in my opinion you probably have sufficient risk tolerance to be a franchisee.

If you answered False to one or more, stop and reconsider your motivations and beliefs when it comes to the risks involved in franchising.

Here's a bit more detail about some of these factors. See if they sound like you or not.

Money is Like Doritos: We'll Make More

Many entrepreneurs have made money, lost it all, made it all back, lost it all, and made it back again. They are naturally not fearful of running out of money because they know they have a skill. Just like some people who can grow great tomatoes, entrepreneurs have a way of growing money when most people can't. That's why they can risk losing it. If they lose it, they'll just make more.

That was the case with Jason Robbins, CEO and founder of ePromos Inc., a promotional products company in New York. Jason started ePromos in his living room in 1997. The company now has sixty-five employees and annual sales of more than $25 million.

I asked Jason to tell me about the darkest days of his company. "We wanted to raise money to grow, that was what everyone was doing [around 1999–2000]. We got in bed with young, inexperienced venture capital guys. We were losing money, but that was what you did. We had no controls in place, no management that understood the business or the drivers.

"As an entrepreneur, I didn't know how to put together a true management team in the face of a tough job market and VCs with demands. I was burned out. When push came to shove, I had to take the baby back, focus, and get serious. Financially, we had no choice but to return to the old days."

Jason had to go through the very hard process of wrestling the company back from its investors, drastically reducing the workforce to skeletal size, and virtually starting over.

He did it, and today he is very much in control of a mature, thriving business with the battle scars to prove it.

This ability to come back (some would say to come back from the dead) is a critical skill of entrepreneurs. It gets so dark sometimes you can't see your entrepreneurial hand in front of your face. Sometimes it is easier to give up and get a real job working for someone else. But it's at moments like the one Jason faced that you find out if you really are cut out to be an entrepreneur.

Don't Blame the Franchisor

Within any franchise system, there is a bell curve of relative success. A small minority of franchisees appear on both ends. There are those who are very successful or very unsuccessful, and there is the 80 percent in the big middle. If you end up on the low end of the curve, I'm sorry to inform you, it's your fault, not the franchisor's fault. You settled for a bad location, you signed a bad lease, you didn't have the talent to be an entrepreneur, you didn't have enough cash, and your bad attitude translated into bad customer service.

Conversely, if you are extremely successful in your franchised business, it actually has very little to do with the franchisor. All they gave you are the raw materials for a business. The rest is your doing. You are just the kind of person who is attentive to the smallest detail, infectious with your enthusiasm for the business, tireless in solving problems, and creative in exploiting opportunity. That doesn't come in a franchise kit. It can be coached and nurtured, but if you don't have it in your DNA, you aren't going to learn it or buy it.

The Thrill of Defeat

Someone who has never had a reversal in his or her life is going to have a hard time in a start-up business. Despite how it may seem, there are those people out there who have led charmed lives. These are the kinds of people who perhaps have a PhD (Papa has Dough).

Unbelievably, there are people who buy a franchise license and then never start their business. They literally walk away from their investment. When this happens, it's usually someone who hasn't worked very hard for that money. I have known two people personally who bought a franchise and then never did anything with it. They just allowed themselves to be terminated by the franchisor for "abandoning" their business. In one case, a wealthy parent paid for the franchise license, and the daughter had no skin in the game. She was a dilettante who wanted to play Barbie Entrepreneur Dress-Up. That was one expensive Barbie doll, Dad.

If you have seen some hard times or had a business failure and those experiences didn't kill you, then indeed they made you stronger. Maybe you didn't rise up from a business failure. Maybe you had cancer and recovered. Perhaps you went through a divorce and recovered. Or even suffered the death of a spouse or a child and recovered.

The recovery lessons will be important as you take on a business challenge. The point is you have to have some place inside you that you can reach down into when things look very bad, and not give up.

You Are Your Best Stock

If you honestly would rather invest in yourself than anything else, that's a good sign of potential entrepreneurial instinct. But most people don't really mean this. They say it as part of a system of rationalizing their decision. For most, if I offered them a 10 percent annual return on their initial outlay forever (hey, sounds like Bernie Madoff!), they'd take that deal instead.

Those are some of the introspective questions you can ask yourself about your appetite for risk. But let's say you are squeamish about risk and want to get a little brassier about it. What can you do to build up your risk-tolerance muscle?

Try the exercise that follows.

An Exercise to Build Your Risk Tolerance

What's a risk vs. a calculated risk, and why is the difference important? When you run a yellow light to avoid a red light, that's a risk. You are assuming no oncoming vehicle and no police car is waiting for you. You may think you've properly assessed risk, but all you did was act on impulse. A calculated risk in the same situation would be to consider carefully whether the fifteen seconds of potential time saving is worth a hefty fine and potentially higher insurance costs or even the risk of death (yours and/or others). Other uncalculated risks could be the time you drove 90 mph in a 40 mph zone, stole a pack of gum from the candy store when you were a kid, or climbed up on the ledge of a highway overpass just for fun. (I cried in horror when my twin brother did just that when we were ten years old).

So, what were some calculated risks you've taken? This could range from buying a house in a fringe neighborhood, spending money on an educational goal, skiing down a black diamond hill after two lessons, buying an expensive tool that you could have rented, etc.

Write down three times that you took calculated risks and answer what the outcome was each time.

Calculated Risks and Payoffs

Risk	Outcome

Reflect on what you have written and then respond to these questions.

1. When you took risks, were you typically rewarded?
2. When you took risks that paid off, how did success affect your confidence about taking future risks?
3. Were the risks taken worth it?
4. When a risk went bad, how long did it take you to recover financially?
5. When you made a risk mistake, how long did it take you to recover emotionally?
6. What have you learned in this exercise about taking calculated risks?

If you are still concerned that you are too risk averse to be an entrepreneur, you may be encouraged by what Wharton School instructor Marc Kramer had to say in a column he wrote for TheStreet.com:

> *When I graduated from college in 1982, interest rates were in the high teens and companies were beginning to treat employees not as family, but as disposable parts. I watched friends' fathers lose longtime jobs and wondered how they were going to support their families. They felt betrayed, as if their wife had left them for another man. Even out of college, at the tail end of the paternal corporate employer, the real risk-takers, at least from my perspective, were the people who worked for one company. It was like buying one stock and believing that stock was going to grow and support you in retirement. There's little worse, especially for a man, than losing your job, if your self-worth is tied up*

in your work. Your identity is based on who you work for and your position. Being an entrepreneur means no one can fire you. For a woman who wants to have children, it means not totally sacrificing your career. The 65-plus executive who is told he must retire but isn't ready doesn't have to. What prevents a disabled person from starting and running their own business? It's really mind over matter. As an entrepreneur, you get up every day and try to secure as many different clients (sources of income) as you can. That diversity gives you and your family peace of mind. Entrepreneurs worry about designing products and services that make clients happy, but they don't worry about having a job, and they know who they are.[5]

Skill #2. Excellent Salesmanship

Some franchises, especially the more developed fast food restaurants, do not rely on a franchisee's skills as a salesperson. At McDonald's, Subway, Dunkin' Donuts, and many others, success is driven by operational excellence. The massive advertising those chains pump out drives customers to the stores. The franchisee's job is to give the customers a good experience so they'll come again.

But in thousands of franchise concepts, there is no such "pull-through" advertising to draw in customers. Indeed, there may be no advertising or promotion at all, except for what the franchisee does.

In those cases, being comfortable with selling is critical to success. That doesn't mean you have to be a "born sales person." But you can't be the type who runs away from making sales.

Tim Reason, a franchisee of TSS Photography, a twenty-five year old franchisor focused on youth sports, school, and event photography, is not a born sales person. Prior to his franchise, he had a long, well-rounded career in the pharmaceutical industry with involvement in manufacturing, engineering, business development, sales and marketing, and operations. When he was laid off, he started looking at franchises and TSS connected with him because of his interest in photography.

---

5   "Risk Averse? Become an Entrepreneur," TheStreet.com, January 12, 2009. http://tinyurl.com/dzct2s

He found there were "skills I need to develop. I need to have more of a sales focus. I have always been interested in photography and taking really cool pictures that someone will want to see. But this is not about cool pictures. This is about going out and getting sales.

"I have to get in front of people, getting sports leagues to sign up, or it will not happen. I've always hated cold calls, but it's an aspect of the business I have to get good at," Reason said.

Fortunately for Tim, he understands the importance of developing his comfort level with sales. Many other less insightful franchisees bury their heads in the sand hoping customers come find them.

Jeff Lutton, who with his wife Sandy is a franchisee of Dogtopia, had a base of sales experience on which to draw when he started his franchise. He had been director of sales for a telecom company and had always wanted to own his own business. After a long and successful sales career, a $400,000 investment to get the business started was a reasonable risk. Since opening the dog daycare and grooming business in September 2007, "everything has gone way past our expectations. We've had to throw away the business plan twice," Jeff says.

When asked why the business was succeeding, Jeff didn't hesitate to answer. "My sales background. I was really good at my job in telecom, and really good at recruiting top sales talent. I knew every top salesperson at all my competitors. I've taken that philosophy over here. I recruited a couple of really good managers and have empowered them to make decisions."

Not everyone who buys a franchise or starts a business has a background in sales. There are tens of thousands of former engineers, IT professionals, non-profit executives, and other non-sales types now in business. There is not a single franchise or business out there that does not involve selling.

So how can you build your sales muscles if you've never used them before? There are a couple of ways.

Sales Training

Early in my career, I was a journalist for business newspapers. The salespeople were on another floor, and when they came snooping around the newsroom, we would all give them the death stare. We hated salespeople. We were pure-as-driven-snow newspaper reporters out to break industry scoops. If we could embarrass an advertiser while doing so, that was a bonus.

It wasn't until I became a magazine publisher in charge of the sales force and meeting sales targets that I began to appreciate who was buttering my proverbial bread. I am not a natural-born salesperson, so I had to learn how to become one. My employer at the time was very far-sighted in terms of developing people and sent me to every conceivable sales training course. I continue to look for opportunities to take sales courses every few years.

One of the best fundamental selling courses I've found is Sandler Training, which is a franchise (www.sandler.com). There is likely a Sandler training consultant in your area and you should look them up. They all train on the same sales premise—get in front of prospects, form relationships, and get a yes or no (not a maybe) to your sales proposition. Most people who lack a sales background spend their lives in "maybe land," where prospects keep you hanging on the (false) hope that they may someday buy from you. They do this by never giving you a straight, "No, I am not interested." They say, "Maybe. I'll think about it," because they don't want to hurt your feelings. Or they like being taken to lunch. Learn how to solicit no by taking a Sandler course, and you'll be far ahead in your development as an effective salesperson.

Other courses in sales are offered by groups like American Management Association (www.amanet.org) and by many community colleges. And don't forget Dale Carnegie (www.dalecarnegie.com). There are also countless books on selling, but I support the idea of taking a course, it makes you spend some money and focuses your attention on developing this essential skill.

Don't ignore the books though. One of the best recently is *The Contrarian Effect* by Michael Port and Elizabeth Marshall. The core of the book is that selling is all about forming and nurturing relationships. It's not about what you are selling. Most people who are new to sales just want to push as much of their product out the door as soon as possible and can't wait for the customer to shut up so they can tell their own story. You'll learn through this book to slow down and let the customer sell himself by showing you can listen and respond to his exact needs and the right time.

Networking

To be effective in sales, you have to be a good networker. I attended weekly meetings of a local Business Networking International chapter (www.bni.com) for about a year. No matter what business you are starting, you need to get out from behind your desk and meet people face-to-face.

BNI is a good introductory platform for networking, although it may drive you a bit crazy in the end because you are talking with many of the same people week after week. However, the underlying principle of BNI is very powerful: it's called Givers Gain. The idea is that people who give a referral to someone else receive referrals back, and it works.

There is something great about being able to help another person in business, even without considering your own needs or expecting a *quid pro quo*. When you think of others, others will think of you, it's that simple.

The BNI folks will tell you that it's critically important to know exactly what a great referral for your business would be. If your customer can be anyone, you will never get referrals. If you are specific about your target, referrals are going to show up. So check out BNI, LeTip International (www.letip.com), or other leads groups.

Skill #3. An Independent Temperament

What does it mean to be temperamentally suited to being a successful franchise entrepreneur? One of the chief characteristics of entrepreneurial success is the ability to think and act as an individual with a high degree of independence. All successful entrepreneurs are contrarians to one degree or another. They are not followers of the pack. Followers, by definition, get low returns and compete for leftovers. They can survive off what others leave behind. That is not the role model for entrepreneurs.

Some franchise professionals say that franchisees are not entrepreneurs. "The person who came up with the concept, and invented the franchise system for that concept is the entrepreneur. Sorry to disappoint you, Mr. or Mrs. prospective franchise owner," says one blogger.[6]

---

6   "Are Franchise Owners Entrepreneurs?" The Franchise King Blog, April 6, 2009. http://tinyurl.com/cvh5gx

Franchisees are supposed to be obedient and compliant. Just follow the instructions. It's like baking a cake! Add water and stir. Does anyone really believe that? I contend that being a successful franchisee requires no less entrepreneurial talent and skill than it takes to start any other kind of venture. To make it as a franchisee, you need a healthy amount of stubbornness and independence.

Prior to purchasing a franchise, I took a psychological assessment required by my franchisor. Of all the people who had ever taken this assessment, I was in the ninety-ninth percentile in terms of independence. This concerned my franchisor because they felt I might buck the system and be hard to control. They worried that I might develop new systems if I didn't like the franchise model, thereby creating management difficulties for the franchisor. They were 100 percent right (more about that later).

Franchisors want you to score about 60 percent on the independence scale: enough to figure things out on your own, but not so much that you want to mess with the franchise's operating procedures.

It is often said that when you buy a franchise you are buying an "operating system," so you do not have to create one. That is true. Neither you nor I are going to improve on the efficiency of hamburger production at McDonald's. The best franchises have time-tested methods of marketing and operations. That, plus brand-name recognition is why most people buy franchises rather than starting a business from scratch.

But there is no rule that says you must abdicate your instincts to survive in business because you are a franchisee. Or that if the franchise model isn't working, you shouldn't look for a way to adjust it. Yes, your franchise agreement says you must operate within the confines of the franchisor's prescribed policies, but that doesn't mean you should not find a way to change what needs to be changed.

You have other agreements that are even more important than your franchise agreement, like your agreements with your spouse and children, with your mortgage company, with the face in the mirror. Those agreements matter, too. Even though your franchisor will position itself as your support system, when things get squirrely, they will look out for their own interests, so you had better look out for yours.

This concept brings us back to the idea of an independent temperament. I think my own example illustrates well the importance of maintaining an independent streak even as you are part of a franchise. If there is one thing I learned, it is this: be very cynical. Pretend you're from New York. You must remain objective and independent, and anticipate changes that may occur in the business environment.

How much flexibility will you have in how you operate if the game changes economically? How convinced are you that your franchisor will be flexible enough to allow you to respond to market changes? I will write more extensively about maintaining objectivity later on.

My franchisor has been extremely flexible, which is why I'm still part of their system and glad I am. I give them credit for awarding me a franchise even though they knew from the get-go that I'd give them some trouble along the way.

My smoothie and coffee franchise was conceived as a retail event business. We sold our products to consumers at fairs, festivals, stadiums, arenas, convention centers, and other environments that featured a high density of potential consumers in a relatively condensed time. I operated within this model for about three years.

Because I have a deep background in sales and marketing, I was able to convince the New York Yankees to give me a location in Yankee Stadium. I soon developed other locations including the largest indoor track and field center in New York, a prime convention center in Manhattan, professional baseball parks and hockey arenas in Connecticut, Long Island, and New Jersey, as well as events like the prestigious Hampton Classic Horse Show in Bridgehampton, New York.

The business model for all the venues was pretty much the same: the establishment took a percentage of revenue in lieu of rent. So for example, my "rent" at Yankee Stadium was 50 percent of sales. That's a lot, but we still did well because we were the only place in the stadium where people could buy a hard liquor cocktail without going to the private Yankee Club. At eight dollars a pop, we sold a lot of piña coladas.

After two seasons, the Yankees saw that I was doing a bit too well. They decided I should pay $35,000 a year in sponsorship fees in addition to the 50 percent of sales they were taking. I bowed out and they brought in another smoothie brand, which turned out to be a disaster run by incompetent operators. The Yankees invited me to come in to the new Yankee Stadium. This time they wanted 95 percent of the revenue (not a typo) and a sponsorship fee of $1.4 million over seven years. I told them I'd get back to them! While not every venue was as pricey as Yankee Stadium, they all wanted more and more. It occurred to me the underlying business model wasn't working well enough for me and would not improve, no matter what venues I found.

The event business also had its ups and downs. We could sell smoothies to Hamptonites who happily plunked down $10 for a fruit shake that cost $1.50 to make. But there were years when it rained for six days straight, and we still had to pay our $1,000 fee, regardless of whether we made any sales.

Some franchisees were coming to the same conclusions that I was about the precarious nature of the event and venue business and started opening fixed location retail stores in malls, shopping centers, and downtown locations. Most soon learned that you have to sell an awful lot of smoothies and lattes to pay the rent. A lot of them closed. Some people lost their life savings. Many are still toughing it out, and I hope they'll prosper.

My conclusion was this: we had a superb product but a business model that, at least for me, wasn't working the way I needed it to. When I bought my franchise, I knew the franchisor was not well known in terms of its brand and had a rather short operating history as a franchise. But I considered those factors pluses, not negatives. To me, it meant I could teach them something as well as their teaching me, and that they'd be open to change.

Once I decided to shift the orientation of my business, I took a radical turn with the business model, aiming it exclusively at catered events where my fee is predetermined and weather-related risk is eliminated. I set my price based on the value of my service instead of the number of drinks served.

I also provide the highest level of customer service to guarantee repeat business. I maintain close relationships through telemarketing, personal visits, e-mail marketing, and other means that are the secret sauce of my success. Today, I have hundreds of repeat customers ranging from colleges to corporations to private individuals.

There's a funny video on the Internet that quips, "When God gives you lemons … find a new god!" That's my philosophy. A franchise entrepreneur needs to know when it's time to change the game in order to stay in business.

Despite my rejection of my franchisor's core business model, they followed me into the catering segment. I sourced new equipment needed to serve the catering market, which they approved and made available to the rest of the franchise network. I wrote the training manual for catering and personally trained scores of incoming franchisees on how to succeed in this niche.

With the support of the franchisor, I continue to mentor and coach franchisees. After all, they want their franchisees to stay in business so they can continue to purchase product. It just turned out that my way, at least for some franchisees, was better than the original model or at least an important addition.

I credit my success to that 99 percent I scored on the independence test. There is no one who can tell me anything when I decide to take a course of action. Just ask my wife.

My dad likes to tell the story of when he took my brother and me to our first Mets game at Shea Stadium when I was eight years old. No sooner had the starting lineups been announced than the skies opened up. Everyone ran for the concourse ... except me. My dad leaned over and said, "Mitch, there's not going to be a game today. It's raining."

I replied, "It's *not* raining."

We sat there for a good long while in soggy silence—my dad, my brother, and me.

As I was saying, to be successful as a franchise entrepreneur, you need to be annoyingly unapologetic and fiercely independent.

That independent streak has also served Laura Lewis well. Laura is a franchisee of Batteries Plus in Idaho Falls. "To be successful in franchising, you have to be the boss," she says. "You can't assume someone at corporate headquarters is going to do any part of the job for you. There might be someone in the real estate department who's supposed to be responsible for leases, or someone in advertising who's supposed to put together promotional material. But ultimately it's my job to make sure those things get done."

Her point is critical. Many franchisees in hundreds of franchise systems believe that "headquarters" is going to take care of things. Well, maybe. They're supposed to provide basic services, like promotional material, distribution, and operational support. But what if they don't do it, or do it poorly, or not in a timely way? Do you think you'll get your money back? Not likely. It will ultimately be up to you, and you need to use your wits to be successful.

Laura, like Jeff from Dogtopia, and like me, was very comfortable with sales and financial planning. When she went to training, "I felt I was ahead of ninety percent of the other franchisees. I went to discovery day with a location in mind. I knew where to get funding. I wasn't waiting for people to do the planning for me. You have to be the one driving your own success."

In other words, you have to be no less independent and self-directed than an entrepreneur who is starting a *non*-franchised business. This trait can be at odds with the personality trait that involves being a bit of a follower. Franchisors like people who can follow a system unquestioningly, religiously, zealously. That's fine when the system is developed to a point of perfection (McDonald's) but is not as helpful when the franchisor is not as mature.

Skill #4. Great Negotiating Ability

The reason you need to be a good negotiator to be successful in business is if you negotiate well—that is, you and your negotiating partner both come out with a good deal—you will sell more, spend less, and potentially have higher profits to sustain your business long enough so that it can reach adulthood. Many people start businesses and are much too quick to accept cost burdens that can have far-reaching impacts:

- If you negotiate to purchase an existing business, and you overpay, you could be saddled for years to come with higher loan payments.
- If you borrow money to fund your start-up and you don't negotiate the interest rate but just accept it as if the bank is a deity of some kind, you will pay thousands of dollars more over the life of the loan. Before you sign any loan agreement, play around with the loan calculators at BankRate.com. For example, let's say you borrow $100,000 and the bank offers 7 percent for fifteen years. You will pay $61,789 in interest. What if you could shave one-half percent off that rate? You would then pay $56,799. Is five grand worth negotiating for?

For a business that makes a 20 percent pre-tax profit, $5,000 is the equivalent of $25,000 in sales. If you don't think that's important, you will not be a successful franchisee.

- If you sign a retail lease and could have done just a few hundred dollars a month better by negotiating more, the affect of that burden will haunt you for five to ten years.

- If you don't absolutely hammer the car dealer who sells you the vehicle you will use for business, you are a sucker. This is the one place where you can and should arm-wrestle the dealership almost to the point of them throwing you out. If the dealer is smiling at the end, you did a bad job.

How to Improve Your Negotiating Skills

The best negotiator I know is my friend Oakley Gentry, who was one of the biggest retail boat dealers on Long Island for more than twenty years before he sold his business.

There are a number of tricks to become a better negotiator quickly. Here's what Oak recommends you do. His advice is centered on the importance of talking less, listening more, and letting silence happen. His advice can be adapted to almost any negotiating situation.

1. Interview the prospective client. Always be kind and nurturing. Ask for permission to ask a few questions. Listen.

2. Qualify the buyer. Make sure the decision maker is in a position to commit.

3. Find the pain. People buy to satisfy a need. Ask, "When you say X, what do you mean?" Ask them to explain their pain.

4. Talk about budget. Figure out how much they are willing to spend.

5. Fix the pain. Ask the buyer, "What would you like to do now?" It's decision time. Be silent. Let the buyer commit.

6. Negotiation. Ask the buyer, "When you say the price is too high, what do you mean?" Be silent.

7. Work it out. Close the deal.

8. Post close. Ask the buyer, "Are you okay with the transaction?" Surface any lingering issues and address them so the deal doesn't become undone.

Believe me, if you can become as good a negotiator as Oak, your business worries will be over. To Oak's expert advice and eight-step process, I add three more steps.

9. Slllllooooooowwwwwww Dooooowwwwwwwwnnn. Good negotiating requires patience. Oak has an uncanny knack for being able to remain silent when most people get verbal diarrhea when they negotiate. Focus on saying less and doing less. Also, slow down all the random saying and doing. When I first started in my coffee and smoothie catering business, I'd get a call from a party planner or caterer that would go something like this:

[*Phone rings.*]
ME: [*Cheerfully, hey the phone's ringing!*] Hello, this is Mitch!
HER: [*Sounding in a hurry*] Hi, I'm calling for a price for a party we're having next month. We're interested in an espresso bar. I see from your Web site that you do that. Are you available May twenty-third, and how much does it cost?
ME: Thanks for calling, I'd be happy to help you. Our prices start at … uh … five hundred dollars for two hours of service.
HER: Wow, that's really expensive. We're only having fifty guests. Can you do it for less?
ME: Uh … sure, how much is your budget?

Duh! How dumb I used to be. I was so thrilled to get the call; I didn't follow a system that kept me in 100 percent control of the negotiation. I often forgot to ask who was calling, to get background information on the caterer or the event, and to qualify the prospect to see what was most important to them in making this purchase decision. I just wanted to get a yes and put an end to my anxiety.

I surprised myself with my incompetence, because in my former executive career, I was very adept at sales. But in previous times, I was not working for myself. I was working for a corporation. Yes, I was compensated based on sales results, but it is still not the same as when the whole enchilada is yours. It takes a re-learning to get your bearings on the sales process once you are doing it for you and not "The Man."

In my new business, out of necessity, I developed simple tools to help me slow down the sales process: a Qualification Form that has to be completed before I will discuss details of our pricing, for example. If people say, "I just want a quick quote," I am very comfortable letting them know I can't give it to them until I have all the information I need.

I also stopped quoting prices on the phone. I will only quote prices in an e-mailed document, so I have a record of what I told the person. My process frustrates some people, but it only slows things down for a few minutes. As soon as I'm off the phone, I organize my thoughts and e-mail them the information they need.

If they can't live with my process, I have to tell them respectfully that I may not be the best person for the job. I've only had to do that a few times, and you know what? It feels good to tell someone who doesn't do it my way to get lost! (Politely, of course.)

10. Call a Time-out. In a seminar on negotiating that I took from a superb marketing consultant, Rennie Crabtree of Marketing Outcomes (www.marketingoutcomes.com), I learned the technique of leaving the scene of the negotiation when necessary.

You can call a time-out for yourself. You can postpone. You can get up, leave, and come back in fifteen minutes or another day. There is no pressure except what you create.

So the next time you find yourself in an uncomfortable negotiating spot, consider removing yourself from the situation. Going back to your neutral corner to consider your next set of moves is nothing to be ashamed of, in fact, it is a remarkably effective tactic for winning concessions.

11. Stop Negotiating with Yourself. How many times have you been in a negotiation during which you or the other party starts making concessions before they are demanded? I used to do this myself.

In my franchise business, we would often provide our product for an event and offer a percentage of sales to the event producer in lieu of paying a fee. If I thought that the going rate was 40 percent for a place like Shea Stadium (former home of the New York Mets baseball team), I offered 40 percent. I anchored myself into a high-cost predicament because I made the assumption that to offer less would have been an insult to ARAMARK, the food service company in charge of concessions at the ballpark. Why was I concerned about not insulting ARAMARK? Believe me, they insulted us plenty once we were in the stadium! And we didn't stay long because the percentage was so high it didn't enable us to make a reasonable profit.

Had I started at 20 percent, I might have done better than I did. So no matter what negotiation you are in, don't worry about insulting the other party with a low offer—as long as you can justify why it's a fair offer. If the negotiation can't end in a fair solution where everyone gets something valuable, you should walk away.

It takes practice to make good deals—some people (like Oak) are natural-born negotiators. I am not one of them. I've learned it the hard way. I hope you can learn it too, the easier way.

Skill #5. Getting the Best from People

Entrepreneurs are often the types of people who think incredibly fast and know exactly what they want. They are capable of doing a great deal of work completely on their own, and oftentimes, even as their business grows, they develop a work style that has them doing too much of everything.

One of my favorite entrepreneurs is Jamey Bennett, founder of LightWedge, Inc. If you read, you know what a LightWedge is. If you read a lot, you have more than one of these gizmos, which illuminate the page of a book better than any device available.

I've known Jamey for many years. We worked together at LendingTree, Inc., where he was the cofounder and head of strategy, and I was president in the very early days of the company. He has sold millions of LightWedges since banging out a prototype in his garage a number of years ago.

I asked Jamey to describe his biggest challenge as an entrepreneur. "I don't do a good job helping people figure out what tasks to do on a day-to-day basis. I tend to define the destination and expect people to figure out all of the steps to get there. I have an unrealistic expectation that everyone thinks as I do, so they will figure out how to get to the destination on their own. Lately, I have discovered that this approach has its limits.

"The thought of having to say, 'first, turn on the fryer, next put one bag of frozen fries in the wire basket, next drop the basket into the hot oil, next wait three minutes for the beep,' really makes me impatient. I know I need to draw a few dots for people to connect, but I am really bad at it. This pattern of mine isn't fair to people and isn't particularly good for business. I am learning to change it."

I have no doubt Jamey has succeeded in learning the skill of developing and nurturing people. He's got too important and successful a business to leave this to chance, and he works on his weak points every day.

There is no more critical a challenge for a small-business entrepreneur than to resist the temptation to do yourself what others can do, even when you know you can do it faster and better. If you hire the right people, you have to focus on supporting them as they learn and improve in their jobs.

There is, of course, more to getting the best from people than learning to delegate effectively. There is an important discipline in organizational management that every entrepreneur should become familiar with—it's called Emotional Intelligence (EI). As part of my coaching practice, I am a certified EI coach. I wish I had learned the skills of EI during my corporate career—I would have been a lot more successful. According to Genos Americas Ltd., the organization from which I received EI certification, EI is a set of skills that defines how effectively you perceive, understand, reason with, and manage your own and others' feelings, emotions, behaviors, and moods. (Visit www.genosamericas.com for more information.)

If you want to understand the impact of EI, think of a time when you asked a boss for more resources when he was having a bad day. Or when you found yourself still stewing about something a co-worker said to you weeks ago. Perhaps you made a decision without taking into account how it would affect the people around you, resulting in a big loss of productivity as you tried to manage the aftermath. Or maybe you confided in the wrong person at work after becoming upset and your angry words went viral through the organization.

Entrepreneurship, whether franchise or otherwise, involves leading by example. You can do no better in this regard that brushing up on your EI.

Skill #6. Displaying Right Behaviors at the Right Time

I have had a close-up view of the innards of a franchise network for more than seven years. I have no reason to believe that my franchise is different from any other when it comes to the traits of the people who make up its base. As I look at the successful and unsuccessful franchisees in my own system, I see clearly identifiable behavior patterns. Compare the patterns here to the ones you noted about yourself in the earlier exercises.

Successful Franchisee Behaviors

1. Walking on the Sunny Side of the Street

There's a franchisee named Ron in Illinois who I have known since I got into my franchise. While he occasionally gets a bit grumpy on the franchisee bulletin board, 99 percent of the time I wish I knew what he ate (or smoked!) for breakfast. He is unrelentingly positive. Whenever I have chatted with him (on the phone or e-mail), I can hear and see (yes, see) his smile. No matter what challenges he faces, he focuses on the positive. He also goes out of his way to help fellow franchisees, offering advice and counsel whenever someone reaches out. It's no accident he's one of the most successful franchisees in the system. He has been in business longer than just about anyone else has.

We all can't be like Ron all the time. (I'm not sure Ron can be like Ron all the time.) So how do you learn to stay positive when reality is slapping you in the face?

Try reading motivational books. A client recommended a book to me and it's a dandy: *S.C.O.R.E. for Life: The Five Keys to Optimum Achievement* by Jim Fannin. The acronym stands for Self-Discipline, Concentration, Optimism, Relaxation, and Enjoyment.

Fannin has coached sports superstars and corporate executives on a system that has to do with reducing the thousands of thoughts that clutter our minds by training ourselves to visualize and focus on a few specific things. He calls this Championship Thinking.

S.C.O.R.E. for Life is a very powerful book, and while I believe that the only system people can truly follow is one they invent themselves, you can select exercises from what Fannin offers and incorporate them into your life. Anyone thinking of undertaking an entrepreneurial venture is going to have to master being in "the zone" Fannin talks about, so if you're possibly headed in that direction, check out the book.

You can also spend an hour wandering the bookshelves of your local bookstore. Go to the self-help section. Take anything that sounds interesting, plop yourself down, and read it. Other people's ideas can have a powerful influence on your own.

Some other ways to stay positive are to make time to engage in activities that make you happy. Business ownership is time-consuming and stressful, but an occasional golf game or taking your spouse out on a date can do wonders for your mood.

2. Talk to Someone

When I was in my early twenties, I had a boss who used to say, "Don't walk the factory floor alone." I was the type who used to brood over a problem. If I didn't know what to do, I hesitated to ask for help. My inaction usually led the problem to get bigger and uglier. If I'd asked someone to help me, I could have gotten more heads working on the problem. What is it about guys not asking for directions?

Consider joining some kind of business group, whether it's a local Business Networking International chapter or a local chapter of a professional association. Let other people know you are struggling. No one will think less of you for being honest. Your sharing will help everyone.

3. Set Time Limits on Brooding

This is going to sound silly, but go ahead and feel sorry for yourself. I did. My business was very profitable last year and my accountant called and told me I had a big tax liability. I was bummed! I made a very conscious decision about this tragic news: I gave myself until dinnertime (I got the news after lunch) to be really good and self-pitying about my big problem, then I would let it go. Evening came around, a glass (okay, two glasses) of wine, a nice fire going, and I was fine.

Later, I felt pretty dopey about lamenting my tax bill when I was damn lucky to have a business generating profits on which taxes needed paying. Nevertheless, as my wife will tell you, I am a high-maintenance kind of guy, and I need to indulge myself now and then. It would be best if you didn't do this at all. I recommend striving to let go of bad news immediately after handling it.

That's what Jim Fannin advocates. I am not a big football fan, but I did watch the 2008 NFC championship game between the Giants and Packers. The Giants' place kicker Lawrence Tynes decided the game by kicking a forty-seven-yard field goal in overtime after missing two other opportunities in the final quarter—either of which would have provided the game-winning points.

So how did he feel going into the third attempt in the most important game of his life after missing the two previous kicks? "I felt good about all the kicks," he said in the paper the next day. "The second one obviously was not what it was supposed to be and I didn't make a very good attempt at it."[7]

Wow, he felt good about kicks that nearly lost the game! And notice how distanced he sounded, almost as if he was looking at it from the stands high above the fifty-yard line. That objectivity and ability to remove himself from the immediate outcome, plus his ability to put a bad performance behind him when most mortals would have broken down sobbing, defines championship thinking. Think about that when you have your next difficult day.

4. Go All-In from the Start

My friend Mary in Minneapolis got into her business at the same time I did and we trained together. She brought her entire family and an assistant to training. She was totally committed from the start.

She used to run a construction company and that experience showed. She was organized, methodical, very grounded, and self-reliant. She's the type you'd want around if you were stuck in a Minnesota blizzard on a camping trip. Mary would calmly figure out what to do so that everyone would survive.

She certainly had troubles over the years, but she clearly comes up on the plus side. "I'm not worried," she says. "My three carts will be booked solid through the summer. I haven't had to look for work for the past couple of years. It all comes to me. Nearly every event or catering job just leads to more work. I am grateful for the work that rolls in,

---

7   "Tynes Confident He'd Stick a Fork in Packers," by Erik Boland, ChicagoTribune.com, January 21, 2008. http://tinyurl.com/dkk4kp

but it has come with plenty of hard work, perseverance, and serving up a quality product with superior service.

"It didn't just happen overnight, but one by one," she says. Every customer and client had to be "won over. I strive to never let them down, never be dissatisfied with their drink or our service. Even in these tough economic times, my customers are still bellying-up to the tiki hut."

Unsuccessful Franchisee Behaviors

1. Blaming Everyone Else but Yourself

You know people like Susan, a franchise owner who sees fault everywhere but in the mirror. She will insist the reason she is not successful is that the franchisor doesn't spend enough money on advertising the brand so consumers aren't being pulled into the store. She'll complain that the cost of the product is too high, much higher than what she could purchase on her own if she didn't have to buy through the franchisor. Of course, the franchisor put her in the lousy location she's stuck in—down at the end of a corridor of the mall.

"They shouldn't have let me sign a lease that was so expensive." Never mind that the franchisor recommended against the location. "Just because it's cheap doesn't mean it's a good location," they told her.

As long as Susan keeps finding fault with the franchisor, nothing is her responsibility. When other potential franchise owners called Susan to ask her opinion of the franchise, she was happy to take all the time in the world to list her catalog of complaints, never once taking any responsibility herself.

While it's completely unproductive and does not lead to success, this is kind of a cozy place to be. You don't have to get up off your keister and do anything. You can sit complacently knowing you are blameless for your failure. Last one out, turn off the lights!

2. Attention Span of a House Cat

A famous circus impresario once said that any animal could be trained to do tricks, except for one: the house cat. He had not seen one of our (four) cats, Cassius, who plays fetch as well as any dog … at least until he starts chasing one of the other cats in the house. If you have an attention span like Cassius, your chances of entrepreneurial success are rather small.

I knew a business owner who bought a retail franchise while he still owned another business that he ran full time. He had a partner who also had a full-time career. I recall asking the two partners which one was going to be in charge of store operations. They said they were going to hire a manager to run it for them. Did I mention they invested $350,000 in construction costs to get the store open? They never actually hired a manager, but they did hire a string of untrained workers who "ran the store" for them. Each partner would show up for a few hours, or a day here and there, but it was mostly the inmates running the asylum.

Another famous impresario said the best way to make a small fortune is to start with a big fortune. That's what these two fellows did. Once they had sunk their $350,000, they proceeded to torch more and more money using various techniques. They tolerated employees who didn't wear their uniforms to work and who could not even manage a "hello" and a "thank you" to customers. They ran a cost-of-goods-sold (COGS) ratio that was 50 percent of sales when it was supposed to be 25 percent. This generally happens only when someone is raiding the cash register.

These "owners" had traits 180 degrees from what they needed to succeed. They had no ability to pay attention to big details, let alone every small one.

3. Not Wanting to Get Your Hands Dirty
You have also met people like Jillian, who love being the boss. She has her assistant do everything imaginable including getting her coffee in the morning, reading her e-mail, charging her cell phone, and calling her husband to tell him what time she'll be home from work.

Jillian is also highly skilled at getting other people to do as much as possible so that she can do as little as possible. She considers her job to be managing others. Delegating is a valuable skill in many lines of work, but in a franchised business, there are fewer bodies around and a lot more to do. It's harder to delegate, especially at the beginning. That doesn't mean you will be fixing the transmissions, but you might be making the donuts for a while.

In fact, you *should* make the donuts for a while. You should learn to make them exactly the way they are supposed to be made, and see all the things that could go wrong while you make them. You should have a standard of perfection for making the ideal donut, and pass that along to your employees so they can make them just the way you want them made.

If you don't know what a perfect donut looks, smells, and tastes like, how are you supposed to train other people to do it the right way? People who are afraid of rolling up their sleeves make terrible franchisees.

If you want to delegate right away and don't want to get powdered sugar under your fingernails, stick to your corporate comfort zone.

Which of these behaviors do you display? Be honest with yourself. It's perfectly okay if you are the type of person who thinks someone else is responsible when things go wrong. Or that you don't have to cause change to happen. However, if that's you, business ownership is not a good fit.

Chapter 5:
The Importance of
Having a Stash

You can play and laugh and fiddle
Don't think you can make me sore
I'll be safe and you'll be sorry
When the Wolf comes to your door.

—Three Little Pigs

If you are thinking of leaving your corporate job to start a business, nothing is more important than having your stash. If you don't have a virtual warehouse filled with your stash when you start your business, your venture will soon fail. If your stash runs out along the way, you'll be stalled on the side of the road in the blazing hot Texas sun with no water, like that drug runner in *No Country for Old Men*. *"Agua, agua!"*

And you know what happened to him.

So, following are five core stashes you'll need to pack for your entrepreneurial journey.

1. Cash Stash

Most people plan to have enough savings to last six months to a year when they start their business. That is not nearly enough. Too many variables can cause you to need and consume your cash savings. That's why you have to have *five* years of cash saved before you start a business. If you don't, just hold on to your dream and start saving like mad. Your desire for a business will grow, and when you have the money, you can make your move. It's not a race!

Mark Cuban, the owner of the Dallas Mavericks, has some good advice for entrepreneurs:

> *Save your money. Save as much money as you possibly can. Every penny you can. Instead of coffee, drink water. Instead of going to McDonald's, eat Mac and Cheese. Cut up your credit cards.* **If you use a credit card, you don't want to be rich.** *The first step to getting rich requires discipline. If you really want to be rich, you need to find the discipline, can you? If you can, you will quickly find that the greatest rate of return you will earn is on your own personal spending. Being a smart shopper is the first step to getting rich. Yeah you have to give things up and that doesn't work for everyone, particularly if you have a family. That is reality. But whatever you can save, save it. As much as you possibly can. Then put it in six-month CDs in the bank. The first step to getting rich is having cash available. You aren't saving for retirement. You are saving for the moment you need cash. Buy and hold is a sucker's game for you. This market is a perfect example. Right at the very moment when cash creates unbelievable opportunity, those who followed the buy and hold strategy have no cash. They can't or won't sell into markets this low, that kills the entire point of buy and hold. Those who have put their money in CDs sleep well at night and definitely have more money today than they did yesterday. And because they are smart, disciplined shoppers, their personal rate of inflation is within their means. Cash is king for those wanting to get rich."*

From the time you have an inkling that self-employment may be your future, you should:

- Postpone all but the most necessary home repairs, even if you are tired of the wallpaper. It stays!
- Skip vacations entirely or switch to inexpensive alternatives.

- Clip coupons and buy store brands. The Stop & Shop Choco-Crispies are just as good (or as bad) as Kellogg's Cocoa Crispies.
- Cancel the Poland Spring delivery—get a filter for the tap water.
- No birthday, anniversary, or holiday gifts for spouses that cost more than a token amount—try writing a love letter instead!
- Keep your old car on the road for an extra year.
- Consider downsizing to a smaller house with lower taxes.

Write five more cost saving measures you can implement immediately.

Cost Saving Measure & Annual Savings

1._____ $_____
2. _____ $_____
3. _____ $_____
4. _____ $_____
5. _____ $_____

Total Annual Savings $_____

Is the total savings you projected at least $10,000 a year? If you're a corporate executive earning $200,000 or more, that might not sound like a lot of money. Trust me; the minute you leave the paycheck behind and own a business, it's a whole lot of money. If you can't figure out a way to save $10,000 a year or preferably more from your current lifestyle in preparation for a business start-up, you probably should continue with traditional work.

Countless businesses have failed because they have run out of money. It's heartbreaking to see this happen. Within my own franchise, and all other franchises, many people leave the business not because they didn't believe it would eventually be a winner, but because they could not afford to get to "eventually."

How can you avoid running out of cash? The best way is not to start the business. What an amazingly simple concept. Just because you think about it, research it, talk to friends about it, and read some books about it, doesn't mean you do it!

Nevertheless, most of you reading this book *will* start a business, and you will need to change your relationship with money. Those two words next to each other—relationship, money—may seem odd. Aren't relationships something between people? That's correct; your relationship with money is all about your relationship with yourself. I'll use my own past to explain.

In my executive days, I had a very impersonal relationship with money. My paychecks and commission checks were direct deposited. I never opened the stubs the company handed out twice a month, and never checked to see if my commissions were accurate. They were large numbers and that was nice. Every two weeks for the paycheck, every month for the commission check. Predictable. Never changing.

Fast-forward. I am in business. No paycheck. No commission check. Bank balance going down instead of up as I spend wildly on (I mean, invest in) my new business. At first, even though I am no longer employed with the last company, I spend as if my paychecks and commission checks will somehow keep coming. Just out of momentum.

After a while, a funny thing happened. I started to notice how very beautiful twenty dollar bills looked, especially when a bunch of them were in a nice pile wrapped with a rubber band. What craftsmanship, what art! Why, I do believe that's President Andrew Jackson on the front! A great president, Old Hickory.

I started to think I'd like to hold on to my Andys a while longer. Andy, what do you say we cook dinner tonight instead of going out? Name your dish. Beef stew? I make a great beef stew! What wine would you want to go with that, Andy? What's that you say? A seven-dollar bottle is often as good as a fourteen-dollar bottle? And maybe just water would be fine, too! Can't be … well, if you say so. Hey! You know, this tap water isn't bad!

Say Andy, the kids' spring vacation is coming up. We usually go to Club Med. What's that? You never heard of Club Med? Maybe we should do what? Stay at home and read to one another, or play games, or do other things close to home and bond as a family? Wow, that's a nineteenth century idea, but I guess I can try it. Hey Andy, Scrabble really is fun!

As an entrepreneur, you need to learn the Zen-like joy that will come from saving money and postponing gratification. When you finally fix that hole in the ceiling and remodel the bathroom, you will admire sheet-rock like never before.

Here's the start of a list of ways to improve your relationship with money.

Have a Money Buddy. Before you spend more than $500 on anything for your business or home, consult a buddy. Do you have to spend the cash today, or can you wait six months? I did not have such a resource when I started out. I bought a $5,000 piece of equipment that I absolutely did not need and could not benefit from. I bought it because the franchisor made the suggestion. It took me six months and a lot of anxiety and aggravation to unload the equipment at a $1,000 loss.

While you are Spending Less, Work on Making More. Your small business can't cost-cut and save its way to growth. You have to create more sales for the business, even as you think frugally. Skip Amazon.com and go to the library (the building with all the books in it— and you can borrow them free!), and check out *The Secret* by Rhonda Byrne.

If Rhonda were an ice cream flavor, she'd be tutti-frutti, but she has an important message. While I can't promise that if you close your eyes and imagine checks arriving in the mail that your wishes will be answered, I do think you can behave in a way that promotes sales even while you are sober about spending. Get the audio tape rather than the book, and listen to it twice. The first time you will be put off by her strange Australian accent and even stranger ideas. The second time (I've listened to it about eight times) it starts to have meaning.

You Don't Need it all Right Now. Our front door was a mess. The lock was busted; the paint was chipped. I hated the front door. I wanted a new front door/entryway. A contractor said we could have a really snazzy new one for $6,000 (and knowing our contractor, I'm sure it would have cost closer to $10,000 when all the unforeseen extra stuff was added).

A few years ago ... new door! Now ... a $20 can of paint and a $200 locksmith visit. And you know what; I really like that new color. I love our front door! For many Americans who were used to having it all, it can be a hard turn to fix rather than replace. But try it. That applies to home repair, cars, appliances, any big-ticket item. Get just one more year, or two, out of them and you will be thinking like an entrepreneur.

Rework Your Family Budget. You really need to get a handle on how you spend money, and the most insidious of all expenses are the ones that come every month in small amounts. We all know the story that if you place a frog in a pan of cold water and then gradually boil the water, the frog won't jump out of the pan. (By the way, I have no idea if this is actually true, and I don't plan on finding out.) Here are some examples of monthly charges to your credit card that deserve a cold, hard stare.

- **Cable bill.** If you subscribed to more than basic cable, get rid of the extras. Once you start your business, you won't have time to watch sports and HBO movies anyway.
- **Netflix.** The library is just as good, and you are already paying taxes for it!
- **Bottled water.** Unless you live in Chernobyl or some similarly afflicted place, there isn't anything wrong with what comes from the tap. Buy a filter if you want, but forget about Poland Spring.
- **Telephone.** Isn't Verizon great? You can have home phones, Internet, five cell phones, and everything else all bundled into one bill … that you can't understand without a PhD. Bundles are the enemy of transparency. You probably have more than you need and definitely more than you can comprehend. Many Web sites will help you find the best deal for telephone service. Give your spouse the assignment of finding the best deal, and make your kids start paying for their own cell phone service.
- **Car insurance.** When you pay your car insurance monthly instead of in one check each six months, it takes some of the sting out. Better to get stung, because monthly billing usually costs more. Get more bids. Take away driving privileges from the kid who insists on not coming to a complete stop and racks up moving violations. Don't buy a new car.

- **Electricity.** Attach power strips to everything, and turn off computers, TVs, and all other appliances that draw power even when turned off.
- **Heat.** Wear sweaters. Turn the heat off when you leave the house. The cats will survive.
- **Air conditioning.** Open a window. Work in the basement. Air conditioning can be a huge expense!
- **Gym memberships.** Walk around your neighborhood. Buy hand weights at a garage sale. Check out exercise videos from the library.
- **Pizza delivery.** Frozen grocery store pizza really can taste just as good for 75 percent less than having Pizza Hut deliver. Stock up when the grocery store is having a sale and use coupons. Costco makes a great ten-dollar pizza, by the way (go with the cheese, not the pepperoni).
- **Credit cards.** Cut 'em up. Paying interest costs you.

If you want to get into extreme cost savings, the best person to talk to is my wife, Stacey. She grew up in a family of very modest means and four kids. Each *week*, each child was given one piece of tin foil for his or her brown bag lunch sandwich. And when the bath soap got too small to use (six people shared one bathroom), it was saved and then all the small pieces were wrapped together in taffeta as a foot scrubber. It really helps, by the way, to have a spouse like Stacey if you're going to be an entrepreneur. Someone who knows how to stretch a budget and doesn't have big needs is an enormous help when you're starting a business.

You can no doubt come up with many more of your own allegedly "fixed" household expenses that aren't fixed at all. In the end, every expense is variable and controllable. If you don't address expenses in the short run though, you won't have a long run.

2. Family Support Stash

At Stash Central, you'll need several tractor-trailer bays to load in all the family support you must have to be a successful franchise entrepreneur. I have seen marriages break up because both spouses weren't firmly behind the idea of starting a business. One spouse indulges the other because it's easier at the time than saying, "No freakin' way are you spending our money to open a Zen crystals store!" Your significant other has to be in for the whole ride. That means if he has to get up at 3:00 AM to make the donuts on a snowy February Chicago morning because you're sick, he's okay with that.

Remember Rena and Keith? Keith's attitude was, "If Rena wants to do it, it's okay with me." After all, her salary was three times his, so she's earned the right to make this call, right? Wrong.

To all the Keith's, may I suggest the following: grow a pair and say "No!" In fact, say "Hell, no!" at least until you are equally as bought into the concept as Rena. More people get divorced over money issues than all other factors. If you and your spouse aren't on the same side in a major decision, how will you withstand all the other challenges your marriage and family will face?

To increase your stash in this important area, you have to realize first that the decision to make a radical change in your life is a heavy emotional issue for your family. (If you are single without any immediate family skip to the next section.) If you have a spouse and children who have lived a predictable economic life for the past fifteen or twenty years, and you are about to indulge your midlife crisis by buying a franchise and turning your family upside down, may I suggest you read this essay my son wrote when he was in high school:

> *Six-thirty a.m … It would be dark out, and I would be snug in my bed. I would hear him leave the house, shutting the heavy wooden door behind him. Hours later, I'd get up and go to school, get home, have dinner, and then get tucked in for sleep. Then, later on in the night, I'd hear the door open again, and heavy, burdened footsteps trudge up the stairs. That was the way of things when I was young. My father used to be the Vice President of a publishing company. He started his work as a journalist for 12 years prior, and worked his way up to the executive level. Quite the accomplishment, but he wasn't happy. And neither was I. We lived a very nice life-style. Upper-middle class at its best. We lived in a house just shy of a mansion, and we went on vacations every year. My mom had stopped working when my older sister was born, so the task of supporting the family rested solely on my father. He*

did an exemplary job of it. And while you might not think it, the cliché "Money can't buy Happiness" was all too true in his case. He hated his job. He hated having a boss. He hated never seeing his family. He was sick of it all, and he had had enough. Then he left his job. This shook the very foundation of my life, as I had been brought up on the philosophy that money was everything and a well paying job was necessary if you wanted to survive at all, much less support a wife and three children. Silently, I began to worry when my dad started looking around for other jobs, jobs I viewed as inferior. He desperately wanted to do something fun, or at least something that wouldn't make him miserable, and would earn a good deal of money at the same time. For a time, I viewed him as a quitter, as selfish; "How dare he quit his job! How will we get by now with no one bringing home money? How can he think that family is more important than money?" Interesting thoughts for such a young child. He went through many similar jobs to the one he had just left, as he began to feel the squeeze of taking money out of his savings just to support us. He left them all after just a few months though, each time coming to the realization that it wasn't what he wanted. Then one night he decided to look into franchises. With a franchise, he could be his own boss, he could make his own hours, he could work when and where he wanted to. He looked at many different franchises, and came across a fruit smoothie franchise. After a few months of research and meeting assorted representatives and franchise owners, he began his new career as a franchise operator. Words cannot describe how ashamed I was. My father, once a proud executive at the top of his company, all the power and authority he commanded, gone. Replaced by a floral Hawaiian shirt, a kiosk, and the 'Aloha spirit.' It was hard for him, as well. He knew he wasn't going to make nearly a fraction of what he used to, yet he kept with it and made it his focus. Slowly, after all the time spent with us at home, he became content and satisfied. He finally had

> *a family that he could see whenever he wanted, and a job to support them.*

Okay, put away the handkerchiefs! The point of my sharing this essay is not that it had a happy ending, but that I caused a lot of unnecessary pain and disruption in the life of an adolescent boy, and his fifteen- and ten-year-old sisters. I didn't consult any of them. There was no family meeting. One day, I just announced that their lives were about to change profoundly. That was very wrong of me, and I encourage you not to make the same mistake.

Family Opinion Counts

If you decide to buy a franchise or start a business of any kind, I humbly suggest you have several family sit-downs at which you present all the facts about how life will change. Discuss at length all the benefits, challenges, and sacrifices you, and they, will encounter. And then shut up and let your family talk. Don't present it as a *fait accompli*. Get honest reactions so that you can evaluate whether it makes sense in light of your family's feelings. Then plan an emotionally intelligent way to proceed, taking into account their feelings and what's in their best interests.

Family Focus Group

Here's a template for a family meeting you might want to have:

- Give everyone a sheet of paper, kids included. Draw a line down the middle of the page. On one side, write Pluses, on the other, Minuses.
- Have everyone write down the Pluses and Minuses of the family being involved in a franchised business. Yes, it's your family that's involved, not just you. The kids' minuses are bound to include that there is not going to be a vacation this summer and other material things. On the plus side, though, they may recognize that you will be home more and there will be more of a family. The idea here is that rather than you presenting all the answers to your family, they get to come to their own conclusions.
- Talk about all the positives and negatives. You do most of the listening and let your spouse and kids do the talking. If you

decide to go ahead with your business start-up, you had better have a plan on how to address the potential negatives they stated. There's no point to having them explain their concerns unless you are going to incorporate them into your plans.

Family Enlistment

Most franchises are small businesses and many are home-based. Most are also more easily understood than the arcane stuff you do for a living now. Your kids never understood the pharmaceutical distribution business you were in, the hedge fund, or the chemical processing business. Now you're thinking about a roll-up-the-sleeves business of your own. Why not find a role for them to play—if not in the business, then at least in the investigation process. Here are some ideas for involving your teenage kids and spouse:

- Identify several franchises and let each (willing) family member do some basic research on one of them. If you were thinking an ice cream franchise would be good for you, have one kid visit the local Cold Stone Creamery and the other a Baskin Robbins and "research" the best flavors. Get them involved!
- Many high schools have business classes. See if your son or daughter can do a project on franchise research as an independent study or for extra credit. See if your spouse/child can work for a day at a local franchise you are considering. Set up a time to do presentations where you can all sit down and exchange what you have learned.
- The point is for you to remember that unless you're single, a franchise is a family affair and that's one of the benefits. So take advantage of it.

So, you involve your family in the process of evaluating the franchise you've selected. What then? Do they get a vote? Do all the votes count equally? My advice is this: *everyone gets an equal vote* and that includes the kids. If you can't convince your kids of the rightness of your decision, how will you convince a customer? If you can't convince your husband or partner, how can you sell what you have to sell to strangers? Your family is your first sale. No sale equals no franchise.

Most people will be able to convince their family members if they are truly passionate about their prospects in a franchise. If you convey doubt and fear, your family, above all others, will smell it. If, on the other hand, you are completely confident and ask for their support and help, and promise them you will make sure this new venture works for the entire family, it's hard to imagine you will fail to convince them.

3. Network Stash

When you launch a business, you need a network behind you, just like in the Verizon commercial. The time to form your network or team is not the day after you buy a franchise, although that's when most people get around to it. If you're reading this in anticipation of starting a business, now is the perfect time to assemble your team.

What kind of professionals and others do you need on your team?

Accountant. The most important is your tax accountant, who should be a Certified Public Accountant (CPA). It is not enough to have your cousin Marty who was good in math do some bookkeeping for you. And the days of using Intuit or other do-it-yourself tax software are over. You need a CPA, and preferably one who focuses on small business. I went through several accountants when I started my business, and it took a few years before I found one that really understood my business and me. For example, I used to spend one very depressing day a month entering all my receipts into Quickbooks and then sending the file over to my accountant, whose bookkeeper would look over the entries I'd made and correct them as needed. We constantly had trouble sending the files back and forth, and keeping my changes and theirs straight. It was an unending source of irritation for me.

When I moved to my new accounting firm, Merl & Hanley of Smithtown, New York, I was pleasantly surprised when Michael Hanley asked me if I enjoyed doing all that data entry each month or if I'd prefer to send his firm my statements and have them do it for an additional nominal fee each month. I nearly jumped out of my skin with excitement about getting rid of this awful chore. I visited Mike at his office a few times and saw a certificate on his wall that states he's a Certified QuickBooks Professional. I have watched him blaze through screens of accounting data on my file with his eyes practically closed. It pays to have a CPA who is also a QuickBooks expert.

Mike's clients are mostly businesses of $1 million and under. This is important, because it means he really cares about small businesses. Other accounting firms I have worked with always made me feel like a second-class citizen. So find out the account composition of the accounting firm you are planning to use. Make sure you can be important to them.

After your CPA, here are some other key professionals to have on your team.

Attorney. Your attorney will help you decide, along with your CPA, on the best type of incorporation for you to establish. There are many choices: sole proprietor, an S Corp., Limited Liability Corporation, and others. If you choose a franchise, you will also want an attorney to review the franchise license agreement and summarize its meaning for you. It will help if the attorney you hire has experience in franchising and small business start-ups, so ask about the relevant experience of the firm or individual you hire.

Business Insurance Professional. You will need property, casualty, and liability insurance when you start a business. Your franchisor may recommend a particular insurance firm that has experience with its franchise, but get at least two quotes to make sure you're paying a competitive rate. You may need to consult a separate insurance professional for health, disability, and worker's compensation insurance—all of which you may need. It is a huge mistake to think you can skimp on insurance or get to it later. One-step in the wrong direction can cost you your house.

Assistant (possibly virtual). When you go into your own business, you will take on a lot of work that if you were an executive, someone else used to do for you. Hundreds of distinct administrative and business activities go along with franchise ownership, and a lot of them are functions that you add no value to as the owner.

For example, if you are doing a mail merge for a direct marketing campaign and you are typing one thousand names into a database, or designing a brochure in Microsoft Word, you are profoundly wasting time. For about thirty-five dollars an hour, you can hire a Virtual Assistant who can do that as well as many other things for you. Check out the International Virtual Assistants Association at www.ivaa.org or call my VA, Virtual Dynamos (www.virtualdynamos.com).

71

You should not be doing any activity that doesn't add value to your business because every minute you spend on "administrivia" is a minute taken away from strategic issues that confront you by the ton, or marketing endeavors that keep the cash flowing in the door.

Nine times out of ten, new business owners will wait until after they launch their enterprise to hire many of the professionals they need. A lot of energy is sucked up on chores that prevent you from accelerating as fast as you really must. Think of your business as an airplane on a runway. You have to get sufficient speed to take off and fly. Your runway can't be lengthened. Waste time and resources, and you will end up ditching. Unload unnecessary weight and your chances of reaching your destination improve dramatically.

4. Self-Care & Energy Stash

Are you thinking about starting your own business after a successful career in corporate America? There are hundreds of important issues to ponder as you prepare to take the plunge. Self-care is one that's often overlooked. This is very tangible, and you can tell instantly if you have enough of a stash in this area. Here are some signs that your stash is lacking:

- You feel wiped out at the end of a work day with no energy left for fun
- You feel like someone has their boot on your chest
- You crave sugar, fat, caffeine, and carbs
- You have aches and pains galore

On the other hand, if people are saying to you, "Darling, you look mah-velous," and:

- If you can't remember the last time you were sick
- If your last vacation was less than six months ago
- If you get a massage, manicure, pedicure on a regular basis (you too, guys—you have not lived until you've had a pedicure)
- If you tolerate nothing negative in your life (that goes for people, your surroundings, everything)

Then you have a huge stash of self-care and energy.

One of my role models for having an abundant self-care stash is my oldest daughter, Jane, who is an actor. She doesn't have a stash of everything yet (money, for example), but she has most of the intangibles down. She needs to or she can't do her job. Imagine Jane having a ton of internal conflict, physical pain, and anxiety, and then taping a TV show like her acting debut on *All My Children*, where she played a flirty receptionist. The audience would see it in a millisecond. In fact, they'd never have the chance because the director would have thrown her off the set. The same is true for you in your business and in your entrepreneurial life. If you are not where you want to be in building your self-care stash, sit down, and write down what you can do—will do—before the week is out to fix the problem.

So, how well are you taking care of you? Many of us grew up with a corporate culture that told us, only half-kidding, "If you don't come into the office on Saturday, don't even bother coming in on Sunday!" (I had a boss who actually used to say this, but always with a smile on his face.)

And if you travel for business, your self-care gaps are bound to be even bigger. The anxiety of getting to appointments on strange streets (pre-GPS), getting to the airport on time, and dealing with issues at home and at the office while you're away, makes many of us feel like there is someone (the boss?) with his boot on our chest. So if you are thinking of getting off the corporate thrill-ride and going solo, you should give some thought to the kind of shape you are in, physically and mentally. You should start doing more self-care at least a year before turning in your corporate ID. Including:

- **Stop smoking.** Do you still smoke? Very nineties. Cut it out.
- **Over 50? Colonoscopy time.** I turned fifty recently and had my first one. What a big nothing! And how great to hear from the doctor that I am in perfect health.
- **Women over 40?** Mammogram time.
- **Caffeine fiend?** Do you drink lots of coffee in the office because it's free and it's always there? Does your generous employer stock the fridge with free soda? Cut way, way back on caffeine and sugar. Life in the self-employment lane will self-caffeinate you plenty. Drink as much water as you used to drink soda and coffee.

- **Check-ups all around.** While the boss is paying for it, make sure everyone in your family has their check-ups (medical and dental) and have as much work done as possible on your employer's dime. (My son needed $3,000 of uninsured dental work a year after I left corporate employment. I could have had half of it paid for with some forethought.) Ditto with eye exams and prescription glasses.
- **Pain management.** If you have back pain or any other kind of chronic pain, deal with it. Chiropractic, homeopathic, acupuncture, whatever may work. Don't go into self-employment without your entire self in great working order. When you leave the office for good, you should feel physically fantastic.
- **Take all your vacation.** If you are really going to leave and it's just a matter of time, why are you pushing yourself so hard? Slow down. Take all the vacation time available to you. Bring no work home. Start to unwind mentally. Do it for a year because when you start your own business, it'll take all the energy you have. I have a coaching client who knows he is leaving his employer in six months, and I am having a devil of a time to get him to focus on his own needs. I admire his loyalty to his employer, but I would much rather see him spend a lot more time on his own self-care.
- **Zzzzzzz.** Sleep eight hours a day. Once you start a business, you'll rarely have a chance to get a full night's sleep, perhaps for several years, so enjoy it while you can. If you sleep more, you'll be more productive as you plan your moves toward entrepreneurship.

5. Time (and Space) Stash

Why do people feel so pressed for time? It's become something of a badge of honor in corporate America to be "crazy busy." (Can we please ban that phrase?)

People who text and talk while they drive must be more important than you and me, right? The talking, jaywalking humans with Bluetooth thingies attached to their ears must lead very vital lives, no? The cell phone dude on a conference call flashing his lights while zipping past me in the right lane at 75 mph is more productive and important than me, right?

Reality check. People who lead lives as if they are in a perpetual Olympic one-hundred meter dash are concerned more with impressing others and covering up their own deficiencies. Life is a race only if you make it a race, and it's really a shame if you do.

Other signs you are a time-crunch junkie:

- You don't stay on task and you frequently can't say what you accomplished at the end of a day, except that you were "crazy busy."
- You are perpetually late for appointments.
- You lose your keys/wallet/purse at least once a day.

All of these are symptoms that you don't have the time and space you need to be an effective entrepreneur. How can you be creative, reflective, and relaxed when you are scrambling? You can't. What can you do to fix the Time Stash problem? A lot. Time management experts talk about fairly obvious things you can do to save time, like checking e-mail only once or twice a day, delegating more tasks, cutting out unimportant or low-return activities, and reducing clutter.

The problem with time management techniques is that they help you clear out time, which you then quickly fill back up, with more stuff. You'll do more "things," you'll feel like you are getting more accomplished. But part of being successful in a business venture is creating time to do absolutely nothing.

I had a boss once who marveled at how many tasks I could accomplish. He got a lot less done than I did, but today he's worth about $100 million (and I am worth less than that). He once gave me a good piece of advice: it's okay to do less. Sometimes, he'd tell me, all you should be doing is bouncing a tennis ball off your office wall (which was his metaphor for thinking). Thinking more and doing less is a very powerful idea that takes a long time to get right.

How can you create more time now so that, should you go into your own business (or even if you already are in your own business), you will be able to focus your full attention on your business?

Here are a few questions that may help you create more time.

How many hours do you spend per week on these activities?

- Watching TV

- Being online for non-business purposes, (YouTube, Facebook, MySpace, eBay, AIM, etc.)
- Around-the-house nonessential projects/repairs
- Playing video games
- Smoking cigarettes (It takes about five minutes to kill a small part of yourself this way and you can't do much else while you smoke because chances are you are standing outside shivering or sweltering while you pull on that Marlboro.)
- Consuming recreational drugs and alcohol

Now that I've gotten you started, play this game with me. List five activities you engage in that are time wasters, then estimate the hours per week you spend doing them.

Now, place a value on an hour of your time. How much is an hour worth? It depends on what you do with the hour. If you put it to another good use, the value could be very high. I am going to put $100 as a basic value of an hour of a potential entrepreneur's time, just to make the point. The value of your time might be higher or lower. Pick a number. Now multiply the hours wasted per week by the value of one great hour and total it to see what watching TV, etc., costs you.

Weekly Time-Wasted Log

Activity	Hours per week	Value of one hour	Cost in Dollars
1.		$100	
2.			
3.			
4.			
5.			

I am not saying that you should not spend time on leisure and relaxation. I wouldn't think of missing an episode of *24*, and when I can keep my eyes open, I sometimes watch a few minutes of *The Daily Show*. And my friends know I spend more than a passing amount of time on Facebook. I know how much time I spend on these activities, and I am conscious of what they cost me. The point is not to kid yourself that you don't have the time do to all the things you need to do. You absolutely have the time. Unless you are President of the United States, you have all the time you need to do everything that's important.

What's even more important than noticing how you waste time is paying attention to spending time in a strategic way. The most successful people I know have clear objectives for what they intend to do every day. They don't let the day just happen to them. They have a list of what they need to do, which they might write in the morning or the night before, and only an emergency will keep them from getting through the list (which won't have too many things on it—only the items that really must be done that day).

Do you have, or can you create, fifteen spare minutes a day? How about ten minutes? If you can do that, you can become tremendously more productive. For those few minutes, you need a quiet space, no disturbances, and no distractions. You need to think creatively about what you are doing. Not in a making-lists sort of way, but in a bigger picture sort of way. Think about whether you are heading in the right direction. What opportunities are in front of you? What threats? What challenges? What solutions? Have one good, clear action step come out of this meditation on your business. You will discover a lot more time to accomplish meaningful work than you thought you had.

Another way to create more time is to clear up the many small annoyances you tolerate. For example, a few years ago, I bought a very cheap phone for my office at Office Max. Sometimes it would charge and other times it would not. For an extra five bucks, I bought an extended warranty so that I could return the phone for a new one if it failed. So, two problems. I have a bad phone, and I can't find the warranty. I created another problem for myself by letting this issue exist for quite a long time—about a year! At that point, totally fed up with the phone, Office Max, and mostly myself, I bought the best phone I could find and the best service provider.

The reason I finally got off my rear end and did this? My coach at the time asked me to make a list of all the things I was tolerating in my life. I wasn't sure why he was after me to do this, but I went with it. Referring back to my notes, (this was about five years ago) here's a partial list of what was bugging me (not in any particular order).

Mitch York's Tolerations, circa 2004

- Not getting enough sleep
- Doing too much heavy lifting work and doing it myself
- Not negotiating deals that were good for me relative to my franchise business
- Hole in the ceiling hasn't been fixed and it's been over a year
- Kids aren't doing chores
- Taking too much money from the savings account
- Don't have enough time to take a morning walk
- Home office is disorganized (and in my bedroom)

I'll spare you the other seventeen items from the list. But that's where I was in 2004 as a relatively new entrepreneur, two years into my business and very pressed for time. None of the things that were on my "Tolerations List" from 2004 is on it today (and while there are still things on the list, it's a far shorter list). By the way, that doesn't mean my kids do all their chores—only that it no longer bothers me as much.

Writing down what you are tolerating creates more time for you because you will start dealing with the negatives in your life as soon as you consciously recognize what they are. Not all of these negatives are directly related to time, but everything is related to time at least indirectly. What's a hole in the ceiling have to do with the amount of time I have? Seeing that hole got me in a funk and distracted me for five minutes to an hour every time I looked at it. I'd go into a mode of compensating for the hole by cleaning a room that didn't really need cleaning, losing another hour. (Humans can be very strange.)

How about negotiating poorly? What does that have to do with time? Bad negotiating equals less cash equals fewer resources available to buy help like a Virtual Assistant to take low-payoff tasks off my plate and an office outside my home where I can work without distraction. Everything you tolerate has to do with time in one way or another. Tolerate less and you will have more time.

6. DNA Stash

A DNA stash? What's he talking about? Somewhere in your hard-wired code, there needs to be an entrepreneur if you're going to be successful. Some people don't have the entrepreneur gene and are better off making a great living some other way. For others, the gene is recessive but can be nurtured.

Here's an example. I went to Columbia Business School with an electrical engineer, Todd. He designed solar panels for industrial buildings. I remember vividly when we took our Corporate Finance midterm. The test consisted of one problem in which we had to use discounted cash flow and other analysis to create a valuation for a company. I got to about Step 14 of a thirty-step process, and then forgot how to calculate the cost of equity. After a minute of trying to remember, I made a little note in the margin: "Professor, I forgot how to do this step, so I am assuming the cost of equity is 12 percent." Then I moved on to Step 15.

Meanwhile, I could hear Todd in the seat next to me, and it sounded like … whimpering. Sweat beaded on his forehead … in the middle of December. When the test was over, I asked him what happened. He said he got stuck after about ten minutes into the two-hour exam, and couldn't continue.

I asked him, "Why didn't you just make something up?"

He was too dazed to answer, but we had a long conversation about it afterward. We concluded that the reason I was able to keep going and he was not, had to do with our core personalities—our DNA. I am a marketing guy, a writer, a salesman, an executive. I make stuff up for a living. He is an engineer. If he makes stuff up, buildings are going to fall down! He has to be right. Once we talked it through, he was able to adjust for his personality and vowed next time to keep going even if he didn't know the answer to a piece of a problem. He got an "A" on the final course and I got a "B." But should Todd be in his own business? Maybe not. Last I heard he was happily designing the most advanced solar panels in the industry for bigger and bigger buildings, and having a great life working for someone else.

Some people just are not meant to be in their own business. There's no genetic test for this (yet), but you can start by reflecting on your own efforts to start up something—anything—that demonstrates risk, innovation, and leading, rather than following. Come up with four examples of when you accomplished something that looks like entrepreneurship, even if you have to go back to something you did as a teenager.

Did you ever come up with a plan to sell your old books to younger kids? Start a club? Design a creative way to sell the most Girl Scout cookies? Beg to work in your family's business and then daydream about how you'd "run" it if you were boss? My coach, Leah, did all those things and she became a successful entrepreneur.

Okay, your turn: what were some entrepreneurial ventures of your own in past lives?

1._____
2._____
3._____
4._____

7. Entrepreneurial Role Model Stash

Just as our parents and siblings are role models for their children, budding entrepreneurs must have role models too. Now, list four role models from your childhood and adulthood who you think are examples of successful entrepreneurs and note what made them successful.

Role Model	What Made Them Successful
1.	
2.	
3.	
4.	

My role model in entrepreneurship is my dad. He came upon entrepreneurship accidentally. When he married my mother in 1954, he was aimless, working at the corporate offices of Sears, the *Miami Herald*, and other places. My mom's father had a deli in Manhattan, so with nothing better to do, my dad started working at the deli and eventually took over Service Delicatessen, located at 1032 Lexington Avenue between Seventy-third and Seventy-fourth streets in New York City. Dad transitioned the business many times, first from an average deli to a gourmet store to a prestigious catering service, and then finally to a party-equipment rental company that my brother took over and built for twenty years before recently selling at the top of the market to the largest firm in the business. I learned a number of lessons from my dad that infuse my entrepreneurship today.

Quality first. Starting when I was about twelve, I went to the store with him every Saturday to work behind the counter, decorate tea sandwich trays, deliver orders, and do whatever else a twelve–year-old could accomplish.

I recall an occasion when one of the counter men was making sandwiches for an order. I remember that the bread was pumpernickel. He called over my father. "Look Jerry, I used up all the bread from yesterday to make these!" He was very proud of himself. My dad glared at him silently for a moment, then swept his forearm the length of the butcher-block counter, sending about two dozen sandwiches to the floor.

"If you ever do that again [use stale bread] you're fired" was all my dad said, and he walked away.

Quality, reputation, reliability, consistency. All of it can disappear from any business if the owner takes his eye off the ball. In my dad's case, the ball was day-old bread. Starbucks' founder, Howard Schultz, knows what I'm talking about. It's not about eggs and bagels. It's about coffee. How easy it was for Starbucks to forget what made them great.

Have an eye for the new. When we went on family vacations (usually the Catskills, Poconos, or somewhere drivable from Queens), we inevitably wandered into food and farmers' markets. While my brother and I squirmed, Dad pored over the merchandise. Often he would find products being test marketed out of the city. Around 1963, he was the first in New York to sell Maxim Freeze Dried Coffee. He found the coffee somewhere in East Nowheresville, Pennsylvania. He asked the store manager how much he had in stock, and my dad cleaned him out. He paid something like 25 cents a jar for a few dozen jars.

The following week, the window display of our Upper East Side store featured this revolutionary product in a pyramid display, selling for something like $2.50 a jar and it sold out immediately.

Another time it was a salty snack called Bugles and Whistles (same snack, different shape). Same out-of-town trial. Same bazillion percent markup. Those corn chips paid for summer camp for my brother and me for years. My dad was the first to have sourdough bread flown in from San Francisco, and the first to have frozen gourmet entrees and *hors d'oeuvres. The New York Times* used to profile him regularly in their food columns. He could spot a trend or a fad—he didn't care which. He saw it as a thick roll of twenties in his pocket every day.

Packaging, environment, and attitude are everything, no matter what the business. Every day the Fink bakery truck delivered loaves of pumpernickel, rye, wheat, and white bread that the driver left by the front door. When the clerks arrived at 7:00 AM, they would slice the loaf of pumpernickel bread into one-quarter-inch slices and wrap the portions in packs of ten, which they would heat-seal closed with a blow dryer. The bread went on the counter for sale.

The loaf of Fink bread cost Dad 50 cents, and he sliced it into about one hundred slices, or ten packages, and sold each package for one dollar. A twenty-bagger in each loaf! Enough to make a venture capitalist proud. Why did it work?

Everything in the store was gourmet. When a customer picked up that package of sliced bread, which set my dad back 5 cents, the bread was viewed against a backdrop of gourmet foods from around the world. The store gleamed. Everything was dusted and in order. The clerks' aprons were pristine white and pressed. Dad could have charged two dollars for that bread!

Let your customers drive your new product development strategy. Phone rings one day and Dad answers. "Yes, Mrs. Rodgers [that is Mrs. *Richard* Rodgers, of the composing duo Rodgers & Hammerstein], tomorrow, five o'clock. Finger sandwiches for thirty. Salmon and cream cheese canapés. Hm hmm. Yes. Nine-hundred Park Avenue, Penthouse One, yes, yes. *(Pause)* Wooden folding chairs. *(Pause)* Of course. Good-night, Mrs. Rodgers, see you tomorrow."

Wooden folding chairs? We don't carry chairs. Yellow Pages ... here we go.

(Dialing) "Hello, AAA Chairs? Deliver two dozen wood folding chairs to Mrs. Rodgers at Nine-hundred Park, Penthouse One, tomorrow, and send me a bill."

Done! Two days later the phone rings. It is Mrs. Rodgers.

"Jerry, you almost ruined my party. Those chairs were disgusting. Broken down and awful looking. If I didn't know you so well ..."

It was that call from Mrs. Rodgers that got my dad into the highly profitable party equipment rental business and eventually out of the food business. All because a Park Avenue woman needed some folding chairs.

The one downside of this experience: it hasn't been possible, in all of Manhattan, to get a really great, melt-in-your-mouth, rare roast beef sandwich on wheat bread, sliced paper-thin, with just a little butter, and a dash of salt and paper, since 1975.

Chapter 6:
Don't Fall in Love
with a Franchise

Ignorance is not bliss—it is oblivion.

—Philip Wylie

It's human nature to rationalize everything we do wrong. Prove my point and complete the sentences below.

1. The reason I haven't lost weight is because…
2. I would have saved more money in the past five years except that…
3. The cop who gave me the traffic ticket was wrong because…

There must be something in the human genome that deflects responsibility for our irrational behavior. We color and shade the truth to make ourselves feel less bad about our foibles. These forces are at play when people shop for a new house or a car or make an investment decision. We let our emotions cloud our judgment.

The same is true when people evaluate a franchise. I did it myself. When I did my franchise due diligence, or "validation" as franchisors call this phase, I spoke to more than a dozen current and former franchise owners. (The franchisor hand-selected four for me to call, and I found the rest in the Franchise Disclosure Document.) Out of the group, there was one individual who I thought had a background, outlook, and goals similar to mine. Most of the people I talked to were at best lukewarm about the franchise and had very different aspirations for their businesses than I had for mine.

I remember telling the CEO of the franchise company that I was purchasing the franchise in spite of, not because of, the franchisees with whom I spoke. I believed I could be successful where others had failed, were failing, or were succeeding on terms that would not have satisfied me.

My assumption that I could succeed doing the same thing they were doing, but doing it better, was wrong. I rationalized my decision because I wanted to buy that franchise. As it turned out, my business has had the highest profit margin of any franchisee in the company that I am aware of. However, it took my complete reformulation of the business model, and a lot of extra time and expense to get there.

What can you do in the course of franchise due diligence to make sure you don't lull yourself into believing you can succeed where others have failed just because you think you're smarter or more experienced? There are a couple of important steps.

Be Cynical

Even if you're from Idaho (I am trying to minimize the number of potential angry letters, so you folks from California and Texas, I'm not letting you off the hook!), you have to be like a New Yorker when it comes to evaluating a franchise. That means don't take anything anyone tells you at face value. Be skeptical. If you don't want to be a New Yorker, be from Missouri. But realize that everyone has an agenda.

- The franchisor wants to sell a franchise.
- Either a franchisee who talks to you in a validation call wants to make herself feel better about the franchise by exaggerating successes, or she wants retribution against the franchisor and therefore trashes it.
- The franchise consultant is a broker who is only paid if you buy a franchise, so by definition she cannot be objective or on your side.
- Your friends and neighbors who you may consult with have their own set of prejudices and beliefs that have nothing to do with your values and potential reasons for buying a business. Some are jealous that you have a new opportunity while

they're stuck in their own personal rerun of *The Office*. Others are afraid you'll trade in the Lexus parked in your driveway for an ice cream truck.

Run the Numbers

Every franchisor requires you to do your own "pro forma"—a profit and loss projection to model your business. They may give you an Excel spreadsheet template to work from, and they may interrogate you about certain assumptions in your model. But it's your model. By and large, they won't tell you outright that your rent assumption is way too low, or your sales number is completely unrealistic compared to the actual results of others in the franchise system.

It's not that they don't know whether your assumptions are good ones—they definitely know. It's because by law they are not allowed to make earnings claims outside of their government-filed documents. Essentially, they have an easy out not to comment too deeply. So if you conclude that rent will be $1,000 a month and they know it will be $5,000 a month, they may ask how you arrived at that rent number, but don't look for them to give you guidance that is much more specific. Likewise, if your model projects sales out of the chute that are five times the franchise average, they may ask you what your strategy will be to achieve the goal, but they won't tell you it can't be done.

Running the numbers is the most important part of your due diligence. The trouble is, by the time you get to this stage, you may have spent weeks or months investigating the franchise. You're already emotionally attached because of the time and effort you've invested. You do not recognize that walking away from a "sunk cost"—that is, money and time spent in error that cannot be recovered—is better than spending even more money and time. You really want the numbers to work out. As the saying goes, if you torture the numbers long enough they'll tell you what you want to hear.

I have seen some incredibly wacked-out pro formas. People have a tendency to underestimate fixed costs like rent, insurance, certain labor costs, cost of goods and other key items. Take Cost of Goods (COGS). Let's say you hear from a number of other franchisees that COGS runs about 25 percent of sales. What they may not tell you is that it settles at that percentage over time and that in the beginning when you are less efficient—literally spilling stuff on the floor—your COGS might be 30 percent. And if you're in a retail franchise, by the time you figure out how employees are stealing from you, your COGS might be 50 percent. I have seen this!

So go ahead and run the numbers for your realistic sales assumption for the first three years of your business. *Then cut the top line revenue in half and the bottom-line pretax profit by two-thirds.*

Can you live with that number? The probability is high that your actual results may be close to that number. Not half the profit you expected: one-third of what you expected—if things go well. And that needs to be completely okay for you to move forward because you may start your business in a slow season, there could be an economic downturn, or there may be some other interruption you can't foresee.

The fact that you can survive if sales and profits are less and losses are greater than you expect in the first few years does not mean that you should change your budget and goals before you launch. It only means that you have prepared for the worst.

You may find something else interesting in the numbers process. Creating a pro forma will cast in a cold light your real reasons for starting a business. For most people, achieving a maximum return on investment is fairly low on the list of priorities because, with some exceptions, franchising is not a good way to make a lot of money. In fact, the best way to make money in franchising is to operate multiple units. Ever wonder how that Taco Bell franchisee with fifty units got to fifty? By starting a couple of stores himself, then waiting for the poor operators around him to get into trouble, then buying their stores for pennies on the dollar and fixing them. That guy is a multi-millionaire.

But let's get back to you and your first franchise. Let's say you invest $300,000 in a franchise. You put down $100,000 in cash and borrow $200,000 from your rich brother-in-law at 9 percent interest for fifteen years (the days of 6 percent home equity lines of credit being history). Family is family, but he insists that the loan be secured using your house as collateral.

So on Day One you start with debt service of more than $3,000 a month. You've also lost the potential interest on the $100,000 down payment, which could amount to a risk-free Certificate of Deposit return of perhaps $300 a month. So you're actually in the hole for $3,300 a month.

Since most new franchisees are first-time business owners, many have never built a P&L model before. Many have never used an Excel spreadsheet. They don't understand the basic concepts of cash flow, how accounting works, or how to create good underlying assumptions. Does this mean they should not move forward? No, of course not. But it does mean they should invest in some advice.

If someone has gotten this far in the process and is basing their go/no-go decision on the validity of their pro forma, they should spend a few bucks and have a professional or trusted advisor look at it. This could be their accountant, or a relative who's savvy in business, or their nephew who's an MBA student. The idea is to get someone to rip apart your pro forma and question every line. How come your revenue increases 20 percent in month four? Why doesn't your labor cost go up even after your revenue run-rate triples? How do you know you can buy liability insurance for that price? What about workers' comp? How much advertising do you need to do? Is the $100 a month you budgeted enough? How come you are projecting a salary for yourself of $50,000 in year one? Do you think that's realistic?

Someone needs to be asking you these questions. By law, it cannot be the franchisor because they are prohibited from discussing anything related to your earnings potential, and all of these sorts of questions deal directly with earnings. So find someone else to do it. It will cost you a few hundred dollars at most, but could save you hundreds of thousands in the end.

There are other hidden costs to beware of that won't show up in your pro forma. Perhaps you borrow from your IRA or 401(k)—something people are more likely to do in the future to finance small business start-ups now that home equity loans are harder to obtain. Then the numbers are even worse because you miss the potential market appreciation of the funds you're using. So you'd usually be better off not buying a franchise if return-on-investment is the only important factor to you.

Speaking of 401(k)s and retirement plans, people are raiding their piggy banks every day the same way they used to raid their home equity. A few years ago, people were buying into franchises by betting on the ever-increasing value of their homes, in the form of a home equity loan or line of credit—and many are now under water on those loans. But never fear, there are always other ways! With a little finagling from a pro, you can get at your retirement plan without tax penalty. Companies like BeneTrends charge a fee, about $4500–$7500, and here's what they do: create a shell corporation and start a new 401(k). Then you roll your retirement account funds into the new account. Through a convenient tax loophole, the new plan can then purchase shares in your newly formed corporation. Presto, your new business is now capitalized.

This scheme is not exactly as complicated as the fancy stuff that brought down Lehman Brothers and Bernie Madoff, but the fact that it's loophole-based should give you pause. Some people will do this and things will go great, or so it would seem. You can read about them in magazines like *Business Week*, which profiles a forty-three-year-old former executive who went out on his own to buy a Nestle Toll House Cafe at a mall.[8] He applied for traditional loans but did not have the collateral and then came upon BeneTrends, which helped him pluck $100,000 out of his 401(k) to finance his cookie shop. The article quotes him as saying, "I took a leap of faith, and it has worked out." Maybe it has, but he wouldn't necessarily say if it hasn't.

Just how many cookies is $100,000, anyway? Let's say his gross profit (revenue less cost of goods) on a yummy chocolate chip cookie is 75 cents. But there's more dough than just dough in those cookies. There's rent, insurance, royalties to the franchisor, labor content, and a partridge in a pear tree. So assuming it pays to make cookies (that is, he is not losing money on each one), let's say he makes a pretax profit of 15 cents per cookie. If the mall is open seven days a week, how many cookies does he need to sell every day to pay back that $100,000 plus expenses and lost appreciation in a reasonable period—let's say three years?

His total investment is $100,000 plus the fee to get the corporation set up, plus his "opportunity cost"—what he gave up in potential appreciation by withdrawing the money. Let's say the total investment he wants paid back to him is $150,000.

---

8   "Need a Loan? Tap Your 401(k), Without Penalty," by Brian Burnsed, BusinessWeek.com, December 11, 2008. http://tinyurl.com/c2ngzv

Answer: he needs to sell ONE MILLION cookies. (That's $150,000 divided by 15 cents net profit per cookie.) There are 1090 selling days, more or less, in those three years. That means he has to sell 917 cookies a day or roughly 76 an hour. That's a lot of cookies! Can he do it? Definitely, he possibly, maybe, could have a potential chance, somehow, I think. Did he do the math before taking the plunge? We don't know. That's not the point. The point is, make sure *you* do the math!

Fortunately for franchisors, most of the people who buy franchises feel that ROI runs a distant second to having more control over your life, being your own boss, and obtaining other intangible emotional needs. As long as those are the priorities of most people, franchises will continue to sell. So run the numbers and don't be afraid of them. Just be real about the truth behind your entrepreneurial goals.

How to Talk to Other Franchisees

When you start investigating a franchise, the franchisor will give you a list of all the franchisees in their system. This list is usually an appendix to the Franchise Disclosure Document or other legally mandated disclosure documents. The list will include names, addresses, phone numbers, and the length of time they have been in (or out) of the franchise. There are a couple of things you need to know about this list and what to ask the franchise holders.

- Talk to the handful of people (usually three or four) that the franchisor suggests.
- Talk to a minimum of six people the franchisor did *not* suggest. Of these, vary them by geography and length of time in business. At least three of these conversations should be with people who have left the franchise.
- If possible, visit personally with at least two franchisees.

When you talk to all these franchisees, it's natural for you to want to know how they like the business, and how much money they make. (Most will not talk about their profits because there aren't any, they pocket a lot of cash they don't want to talk about, or because it's really none of your damn business!) You might want to know whether the franchisor offers good support, what problems they have had, and that most popular question of franchise validation, "If you had it to do over again, would you buy this franchise?"

I have been asked that last question a hundred times, and my answer is always the same: that's a dumb question. Ask real questions, not fantasy questions.

All the due diligence information is great to have, but there is something more important for you to evaluate. You should be very attuned to the attributes that make people highly successful or highly unsuccessful in business and how the people you are interviewing project those characteristics, either positively or negatively. Ask these questions to get past the superficial information.

- **Do you consider yourself a success in this business?** If so, what are the measurements of success? If not, why do you think you have been unsuccessful? These are such better questions than, "Can you make money at this franchise?" With this question, you'll get a textured answer about the values of the person. Do they care most about money, time, or quality of life? If the franchisee you are talking to is successful, asking this question will make him or her think you have something on the ball, too. I have spent three minutes on the phone with some prospective franchisees who are clueless and an hour with others who ask smart questions.

- **What are the key attributes you have that make you successful in this business?** Is that a better question than "How long will it take to break even?" Yes! You'll learn about the person's business ethics, judgment, and values. Then you can compare hers to your own. Do you have the same or similar characteristics that might indicate the probability of your success in the same business?

- **Why did you go out of business?** What's critical here is whether the person takes responsibility or blames others for his failure. Sometimes the reasons for getting out have to do with unexpected issues (relocation of a spouse, health emergencies, etc.) but most of the time it has to do with sales that were too low, expenses that were too high, lack of support, and commitment that wasn't present.

- **What were the most difficult lessons you learned in your first year of operation?** What were the surprises? Listen very carefully here, particularly to the people who sound like successes. The answers to this question can save you tens of thousands of dollars should you buy a franchise. Often franchisees make mistakes that could have easily been avoided—everything from buying unneeded equipment, as I did, to overpaying for insurance and capital leases. Not everything you need to know is covered in training. There's always something missing from the information the franchisor provides. And even if training is excellent, it may only be for a week or two and you'll forget half of what you learned on the plane ride home. So any reinforcement you can get on fundamentals will be incredibly important.

After you've talked with half dozen or perhaps two dozen franchisees, you have a lot of information to process. Remember that you have invested tremendous time and effort into the due diligence process and that it means absolutely nothing. You have spent so much time investigating and talking to people that you rationalize a reason to go ahead despite warning signs to the contrary. Many people fall into this trap. You have to be brutally honest with yourself, and very importantly, have someone to consult with who'll be an objective party as you sort out all the information.

Visiting a local franchisee can be beneficial, even before you begin formal discussions with the franchisor. In fact, you can save thousands of dollars by doing so. Franchisors may or may not tell you if there are resale opportunities in the franchise. Some franchisors view resales as more difficult for them to process, and the franchisor does not make nearly as much money as they do if they sell a new license.

By visiting a franchisee, you can find out whether there may be resale opportunities available within the system. If there are and you can contact potential sellers directly, you can begin the negotiation process before you contact the franchisor. Then, when you do contact the franchisor, you go in with a lower overall cost basis for your business. This can make all the difference in the overall profitability of your franchise. If you would have paid $500,000 for a new franchise, but only $250,000 for a resale that $250,000 savings isn't just $250,000. It's the savings of the ongoing debt service, plus the positive investment potential on $250,000.

How to Talk to a Franchisor

The Franchise Sales Process

In economics, there is a principle called asymmetric information. This simply means that in all transactions, one party has more information than the other has, and therefore has a negotiating advantage. When you buy a car, the dealership has the upper hand. The Internet has mitigated their advantage to some extent, but your irrational desire for the hot new model often wipes out the benefit of your studying online information.

In franchising, franchisors have the asymmetrical advantage. They are keenly aware of the psychological state of prospects that pass the first few steps of the franchise investigation process. Their sales processes have been fine-tuned to take maximum advantage of your interest and vulnerability. Franchisors know you got in touch with them at a propitious time. Something triggered your interest: an event like a layoff at work, or a feeling of insecurity about the future of your job. It wasn't random. No matter what triggered your interest, you are in a highly emotional state in which you are susceptible to their slick sales pitch. Remember Rena? She let her fingers do the clicking in a moment of fatigue and weakness.

Throughout the days and weeks after your make your initial contact with a franchisor, you will be in touch with your franchise sales manager who will guide you through the process. He will position your investigation of the franchise so that you feel you must prove yourself worthy of being granted admittance. You will develop muscles you never knew you had from jumping through their many hoops. For example:

- You must qualify financially by preparing a statement of your net worth.
- You may be required to take a personality test.
- You will be interviewed by several franchisees who will give their input to the franchisor about whether you'd make a good addition to the system.
- The executive team of the franchisor will interview you.
- You may have to visit the franchisor's headquarters at your own expense.

- You will be assigned tasks and voluminous homework that will be due at specific times.

The franchisor will not tolerate delays or missed dates for you to complete various stages of the process, because they are evaluating whether or not you are the type of person who can follow directions and adhere to a business where you will be tightly controlled in many ways.

There's another, even more important, reason they will not tolerate delays. They have a guiding principle when it comes to selling franchises: *Time Kills Deals*. If you can't make a phone conference because of illness, a business trip, a hockey game, whatever, they know that the chance of their closing the deal just fell substantially. Miss two calls and their chances fall to approximately zero.

The franchisor may tell you up front that you will have a "decision-day" in four or six weeks—the date on which the franchisor will decide whether to offer you a franchise and right after which you will need to decide whether to accept it if it is offered.

If you want to extend the date by a month, the franchisor may well deny you and close your file. Why? I just told you—*Time Kills Deals*. The more time you take to think about whether to sign, the less likely you are to pull the trigger.

My advice is that if the decision day is less than eight weeks from the time you contact the franchisor, move to push it back early. Make up a story. Tell them you have a two-week vacation right at decision time, or you have a business trip that will take you out of the country. It doesn't matter. Buy more time, at least a month, the first time a decision date is discussed. If you set expectations early, you're likely to get the franchisor on board with your timetable.

You need to resist the immense pressure you feel during the process because of the franchisor's techniques. They may say that you have to make a decision at a certain day and time. Do you? No, you most certainly do not. If you are a great prospect and you need time to do more research, demand it. If they say no, find another franchise. There are thousands.

The Franchise Agreement

If you are serious about the franchise, at some point you will receive and review the franchise agreement, which spells out the rights and responsibilities of you and the franchisor. It is essential that you hire an attorney to review the document. Some people want to save a few hundred dollars by doing the review themselves, but unless you are a lawyer, you are not going to understand a lot of what the agreement obligates you to do, nor are you going to think about the long-term implications of agreeing to provisions that seem innocuous today.

Franchise license agreements are almost completely one-sided, favoring the franchisor in every respect. The franchisor, through the franchise agreement, controls what you sell, how you sell it, what you can say about the franchise, and how you say it. Also, whom you may someday sell your franchise to and on what terms, how much you will owe the franchisor if you do sell it, what happens to your franchise if you die, where you purchase your products, and the many ways you may be forced to forfeit your license with no recourse.

The franchisor will lead you to believe that not a word of the license agreement can be changed to address your particular concerns. They will tell you that if they change so much as one semi-colon in your agreement, it can expose them to liability because they may not have made that change available to other franchisees. This is true for some things. It's doubtful that you're going to negotiate a different royalty rate on sales than the franchisee down the block. However, many other things you may want are very obtainable. So review the agreement carefully and ask for the moon and the stars. Take up their time and energy. Find at least a dozen things to change that are meaningless to you and ask for them. Then give them up as "concessions" to get the things you really want. If you don't get ready for some full-contact negotiation, you are, to quote William Shatner of Priceline.com fame, a wuss!

Some examples of what you might try to negotiate:
- **Development Period.** Many franchisors specify the rate at which a franchisee has to open stores or otherwise develop their business. Their timetable does not take into account business conditions in your particular market area. If you aren't comfortable with the period specified, negotiate to lengthen it. You have to be really comfortable that you can achieve what you agree to in this regard. If you don't build out your business, the franchisor has a big opportunity cost. They are very likely to hold you to the standard you agree to, and the penalty for not

building out on their timetable could be the loss of your license on unfavorable terms.

- **Renewal Charges.** Most franchise agreements have a stipulation for the amount you will pay to renew your franchise license after it expires. That could be a ten- or twenty-year time horizon. In the adrenalized period of franchise review, you may not be thinking about the terms of renewal so far down the road. But what if you could negotiate the renewal terms and get the franchisor to agree to a lower renewal charge? Or a longer franchise agreement? Does it make sense to ask? Yes, it really does. When I signed my ten-year agreement, little did I know that another franchise right up the road got a twenty-year agreement. The franchisor had changed its policy to go to ten-year agreements, but I am pretty sure I could have had a twenty-year agreement or something close to it had I pursued the point. They might have pushed back because of their new policy, but in the end I am convinced we could have worked out a good solution, perhaps a compromise, because I was exactly the type of franchisee they wanted in the system. At the time, a longer agreement wasn't that important to me. I was, in some ways, negotiating against myself because I felt the franchisor would not concede this particular point. Therefore I didn't raise it. Dumb! Had I gotten this change, it would have postponed an expensive renewal payment due in a few years, and more importantly, lengthened the term of my franchise license so that an acquiring company would have paid me more for it should I choose to sell.
- **Transfer fees.** The franchisor loses a potential sale if you sell your license to someone else. They will charge you a fee to transfer your license. Their actual incremental costs are almost nothing: they need to put the prospect through their review process and generate a transfer document, but that's it. Yes, they have to train that person, but she is just one of many in a classroom so there is no meaningful incremental cost to do that training. For this, they will charge you thousands of dollars. Think about it: there's a reasonable probability that you will sell your franchise before the term of your license is over. So, if you

can, negotiate the transfer fee up front to be less than what the franchisor asks for.

- **Training costs.** Some franchises will include training for one person in the cost of your franchise license, but may want to charge you for having additional people attend training. Aside from travel and lodging costs, which you pay, there are no other significant incremental costs to train an additional person, so ask for it if you want it, and offer to pay for meals and lodging only.

Caveat: please keep in mind that I am not an attorney and all contracts are different, so have an attorney recommend changes based on your specific situation.

How Not to Ignore What You Find Out in Due Diligence

Once you've gotten all the information from a franchisor, then, if you're like most prospective franchisees, you start the process of ignoring it. We all do it, and I'm at the front of the line. It's just like buying a house. Who cares if the roof leaks, I love the backyard.

With me in this queue is my good friend Bob, with whom I went to Columbia Business School. Bob, who graduated first in our class, is an investment analyst and is a franchisee of a specialty footwear and orthotics retailer. Bob had some reservations about his franchisor during the due diligence process. He felt the company's marketing skills and staff were not as good as they should have been, but the company promised it was going to improve in this area.

Looking back three or four years in retrospect, Bob says little has changed. The company still has marketing problems. The lesson? "If a franchisor is having problems in a certain area when you are doing your research, don't assume it will get fixed.

"We go to the franchisee conference every year," Bob continued, "and every year they have a new program and strategy that they will be implementing in the future, which never happens."

Looking back, Bob also concludes he could have been more critical of the financial prospects of his franchise. (As I mentioned, Bob was #1 in our Columbia class—he knows how to run the numbers, backward and forward.) After purchasing his franchise license, he was unable to find a retail location he liked, so after a year of looking, he overpaid to purchase an existing franchise.

"We tried to justify the purchase price based on the replacement value," which is typical of the rationalizing all franchisees do to justify a decision. Rather than using tried-and-true financial multiples to come up with a rational price, Bob overpaid to get into business. It's fair to say emotion played a strong part in the premium he paid. The message here? Even the most astute financial analyst you'll ever meet will, like the rest of us, look past certain critical and available data and later regret doing so.

Choosing to ignore certain information you come across in due diligence isn't just a factor when it comes to your own pro forma. How about the franchisor's? A franchisee I know looked at his franchisor's income statement and balance sheet and thought that the stated asset amount was missing a few zeros. It wasn't. This franchisor was running on a shoestring with scant capital resources. Its working capital was funded largely by selling more franchises. That meant not enough capital to invest in support, marketing and branding, training, opening company stores, and other necessary items.

The result: a franchise operation that can't adequately support its franchisees, and that employs inexperienced, if well meaning, people in critical roles. So if there appear to be zeros missing from the franchisor's income statement and balance sheet, take pause and decide if it's smart to ignore that information.

Beware of the "Agency Conflict"

Bob also noted a concern that franchisees develop once they have been in the system a while. It's what our business school macroeconomics professor taught us, and it's called "the agency conflict." This arises when two parties become partners in a venture and then come to realize they are not really on the same side. All the talk from franchisors about franchisees "being in business for yourself but not by yourself," only goes so far.

Bob was one of three franchisees in town when he learned that the franchisor was talking to a fourth potential franchisee in the market. He and the other franchisees, already facing a difficult market, would likely find their businesses significantly affected with a fourth store in the area. They even went so far as to try to talk the potential fourth player out of starting his franchise and pleaded their case with the franchisor. Nevertheless, the fourth franchisee did open and now everyone has less business. This phenomenon happens with many franchises.

I have spoken to operators of Quizno's, the sandwich chain, who thought they had a protected territory when they purchased rights to a specific town, only to find that the company would sell a franchise to someone the next town over, which could be mere blocks away. This is "agency conflict," and it's up to the prospective franchisee to realize that once you become an insider to the franchise system, the franchisor will be looking out for their own interests first, and yours decidedly second.

Look for Franchisors with Something Extra to Offer

Given the economy today, prospective franchisees can have their pick of concepts. Why not pick a model that offers extra incentives? According to *The Wall Street Journal*, transmission franchisor Maaco Enterprises, Inc., has introduced a money-back guarantee.[9] "If after the first year a new franchisee hasn't achieved a certain sales level despite having operated a 'first-class' business, the company will buy the franchise back. Certain conditions apply, including using sale proceeds first to pay off loans outstanding and any money due Maaco."

Not bad.

Another example cited by the *Journal* is Dwyer Group, which "encourages workers at its various repair and maintenance franchises to eventually buy their own franchise. For example, employees of a Mr. Appliance franchise can get 10 percent off the initial cost of a franchise, which averages around $45,000, if they work in the business for two years and perform well. If they remain seven years, they could get 75 percent off the initial fee."

Innovative!

Maaco and Dwyer are taking on some risk, which is unusual and earns them points. So ask your prospective franchisor what they can do for you if you perform well.

---

9   "How to Finance a Franchise," by Richard Gibson, The Wall Street Journal, March 17, 2008. http://tinyurl.com/ca56ft

Chapter 7:
Don't Buy a Franchise Before You Consider Going It Alone

The individual has always had to struggle to keep from being overwhelmed by the tribe. If you try it, you will be lonely often, and sometimes frightened. But no price is too high to pay for the privilege of owning yourself.

—Friedrich Nietzsche

If you've made it this far in the book, I'm going to assume you really are the type of person who will thrive being in business for yourself. You have a strong belief in yourself and are willing to bet on your own success. You are independent and have ample financial and other resources available. You have a compelling vision for being in your own business, and you are considering the relative costs and benefits of franchising. I also encourage you to consider starting your own business from scratch.

Like anything else in business, franchising encompasses a series of trade-offs. Here are some of the most important considerations. Note that the "positives" below assume that the franchisor has their act together. There are also franchisors that are so lame they can't offer even the most basic services associated with franchising. But for this exercise, let's assume every franchise has the operational excellence of McDonald's.

Franchising Trade-Offs

Positive: Brand is pre-established.
Trade-off: Cost of licensing is high.

Positive: Operating procedures are documented and proven.
Trade-off: Operating procedures are restrictive—you can't do it "your way."

Positive: Distribution is in place, giving you a reliable supply chain.
Trade-off: You may pay more for commodity items and have no choice of using alternate suppliers.

Positive: Marketing materials are created for you so you can focus on your business.
Trade-off: You pay a royalty on sales in exchange for marketing support.

Positive: The franchisor provides ongoing support to help you succeed.
Trade-off: The support can sometimes be punitive; if you fail to do things "their way," you risk termination.

Let's consider some of these factors in the context of making a franchise/no-franchise decision.

Brand Power

There is no questioning the power of major franchise brands like McDonald's, Subway, Dunkin' Donuts, and 7-Eleven. When you and I are on the road, seeing the Subway store around lunchtime draws us in like bees to honey. When we need a caffeine boost, do we question that America runs on Dunkin'? Munchies at 3:00 AM? (Admittedly more my son's problem than mine.) A 7-Eleven is just around the corner. Every American knows exactly what these brands mean.

If you want in on some of these franchise brands, you'll need access to upward of a million dollars in liquid capital and the ability to open multiple units on a timetable of the franchisor's choosing. With others, the start-up costs are less, but the ability to make significant money is hampered by the royalty structures of the franchise.

When it comes to brand power, bigger, more established franchisors obviously are stronger than start-up franchisors. That's another reason to take a serious look at franchisors that have stood the test of time rather than buy into a relatively new franchise.

According to the American Association of Franchisees and Dealers, companies that sell franchises go under at a rate of about 15 percent a year. That means that in any given five-year period, 75 percent of franchisors disappear. (Of course, there are always new franchises taking the place of those that failed.) Even well established franchises can fail (remember Bennigan's?) but the odds are better with those that have withstood the test of time.

Operating Procedures

When you buy a franchise—if it's a good one—you get an "operating system" that is tried and true. No one is going to improve on the volume production of McDonald's hamburgers and fries except McDonald's. If you're a franchisee, they will tell you how it's done based on hundreds of thousands of hours of observation, time and motion studies, and operations research modeling done by the biggest brainiacs in corporate America.

But what if you buy a franchise from a small franchisor like I did? The operations manual was about fifty pages. (It's now about 500 pages.) The value of the operating procedures I purchased was good, relative to the cost of entry. I didn't need millions of dollars to buy the rights to use their system—only a mid-five-figures investment—so I got what I paid for. But I quickly found that a low-cost/low-risk franchise had hidden costs and risks when it came to operations.

With my franchise license, I bought an operating system to sell fruit smoothies at fairs, festivals, and venues such as stadiums and arenas. Here are a few examples of what the operating manual did *not* tell me. I have dozens more—buy me a beer if you want to hear the rest. Collectively, the lack of operating information wound up costing me a great deal of time, money, mental anguish, physical injury, and expensive liquor store bills.

The 900-pound Gorilla in the Trailer

Moving our 900-pound smoothie kiosks from one event to another required the use of a cargo trailer. But there was nothing in the manual about how to specify and purchase a trailer. The franchisor did not have information on how to do this (not in the manual, nor on the phone), so I consulted another local franchisee who gave me the bill of sale of his trailer and the name of the local dealer who sold it to him. I took that information to the dealer and ordered a copy of the same trailer. (I did this before I received my first kiosk.)

I had my first kiosk shipped directly to the site of a weeklong tennis tournament at which we were going to operate our first event. Following the tournament, I would need to move the equipment to another weeklong event fifty miles away. The trailer was ready to be picked up on the last day of the tennis tournament. I picked it up, drove it to the site of the tournament, and proceeded to load the kiosk onto the trailer. My wife and I were pushing the 900-pound gorilla up the ramp and it was getting stuck on something.

I heard her yell, *"Holy S**t!"*

The ramp door opening was half a foot too short for the kiosk! Now, how did that happen? Turns out the kiosk my fellow franchisee owned was significantly shorter than mine was. The franchisor had changed kiosk manufacturers but hadn't let me or anyone else know that. And the new kiosks were a lot bigger. To say this was the worst day of my life (at least up to that point) is not an exaggeration.

Like moving-vehicle stories? Here's another.

As I mentioned, there was nary a word about trailers in my franchise operations manual, which is odd because a trailer is required equipment to move the kiosks to events. When I finally did get a trailer that fit the kiosk, I set off for a destination about seventy miles away. My journey took me on highways, bridges, and tunnels through New York and New Jersey. Tough roads! I could hear a lot of bangs and bumps, but with the noise of New York traffic, I assumed it was all the cars and trucks around me on that scenic of all New York highways and byways—the Cross Bronx Expressway.

I arrived at my destination just off the New Jersey Turnpike and noticed the sheet metal on the outside of the trailer was dimpled in a bunch of places. Hmmm. I opened the trailer hatch and saw that the bungee cords I used to secure the 900-pound gorilla inside hadn't worked too well. The kiosk had broken the side door of the trailer, smashed through the interior aluminum trim creating lots of jagged edges, and the brand new, $20,000 kiosk also was seriously damaged. I later learned I was supposed to use something called a "ratchet strap" to secure cargo in the trailer. Now they tell me!

Eventually, I got very good at trailer driving and maintenance, but there wasn't a mistake that was makeable that I didn't make.   M o r a l of the story: make sure your franchisor has an impeccable operations manual, and ask franchisees about unexpected mistakes and surprises.

Because my franchisor was fairly small and new when I signed on in 2002, its operating system was still in early development. I paid the price with hassles, accidents, and near catastrophes the likes of which I never expected. I have come to be a believer in the adage, "What doesn't kill us makes us stronger." Seven years later, Superman has nothing on me. Fortunately for newer franchise owners, the company has matured and its systems have improved significantly.

What is the lesson here? If you are buying into a franchise that has been around for less than ten years or so, you are likely going to pay hidden costs that will manifest themselves through your operating mistakes. That means your overall investment is going to approach what it would have been with a more expensive, more experienced franchise. Maybe the newer franchise is better for you, but not because it's cheaper. So don't kid yourself into believing there is anything like an inexpensive franchise.

If you are going to spend $250,000 or $1,000,000 or even $50,000 to start a business, do you need a franchise operating system to get you going? My conclusion is that relatively new franchise concepts are incredibly risky propositions, and that if you are buying into one with the belief that all the operating risk has been taken out, you are in for some big surprises. So unless you are ponying up big bucks to buy a sophisticated, bulletproof, franchise operating system, you should at least ask yourself the question: why bother with a franchise at all?

Support

Support by your franchise can be a tricky proposition. Some franchises have big staffs to coach you through all the phases of your business. They have field support personnel who work with you and help you become a better operator. Of course, they are also in the field to make sure you comply with franchisor policies, and if you don't, you could lose your franchise license.

Some smaller, less-well resourced franchises are much less skilled when it comes to support. After all, how is a franchisor with a dozen operations staff adequately supposed to support hundreds of franchisees in the field? Often the franchise support people have never run a business of their own. Therefore, they may not be able to walk in the shoes of their franchisees and fully understand what their franchisees are up against.

You can reasonably expect a franchisor to offer support in terms of how to operate efficiently. If they can't step up in that regard, then you really aren't getting value for your franchise license. But the higher-level of support franchisees need—the ability to think and act strategically about their business and be a constant partner in their success—is unlikely to come from the franchisor. For that, a franchisee or any business owner needs the advice of other franchisees plus one-to-one interaction with a professionally trained and certified coach.

Non-Franchise Alternatives

While there many types of businesses you can choose to start, two stand out as ones I'd suggest you consider if you're thinking about buying a franchise.

Micro-business

The idea of going into business for yourself can come with projections of a lot of investment and expense, particularly if your frame of reference is big-company employment.

It does not have to be that way. There are business opportunities that require very little investment and rely on expertise the owner already possesses. For example, it's relatively easy to set yourself up in an equipment and product repair business. Or, if you have a software development background, you might develop new applications for Facebook or LinkedIn, or become a software consultant.

According to *Inc.* magazine, "The percentage of micro businesses—defined as 10 or fewer employees—operated out of the home has grown steadily since 2005. According to the National Association for the Self-Employed, 55 percent of micro businesses in 2007 were home-based, up from 48 percent in 2005. Home-based businesses count for more than half the estimated 27 million small businesses in the United States."

Entrepreneur Bruce Judson advocates the most extreme form of micro-business-solopreneurship. He wrote a terrific book a few years back called *Go It Alone!: The Secret of Building a Successful Business on Your Own.* In the book, he gives numerous examples of people who have created businesses in little time with almost no money and which create ongoing (and often passive) revenue streams. He argues against buying a franchise because they are usually inflexible, require a lot of upfront capital, and may not be a sure thing anyway. He also is against the idea of being a "Free Agent," or freelancer/consultant, because then you are the entire business. When you are a consultant, you have a practice, not a business. The potential of the business is bound by your time constraints.

Judson sites many Internet entrepreneurs who have found niches to serve highly targeted markets and do so without much competition. If you're self-reliant, good with technology, and like to work unfettered by other peoples' systems, this kind of business could be perfect for you.

Networking Marketing as an Alternative to Franchising

If you conclude that starting a business is the right thing for you, but you do not want to take on the risk of starting something from scratch or buying an expensive franchise, there are other viable alternatives such as Network Marketing, also called Multi-Level Marketing (MLM). Just as franchisors sell their products through a series of franchisees, other companies sell through independent sales representatives. These reps or distributors are unsalaried but receive commissions from the parent company based on the volume of product they sell. They also receive commissions when they sign on others to become distributors.

The cost of entry is much lower in MLM—typically under $500 for a distributor license. But you get what you pay for. A franchise should give you a recognized brand and should attract customers through re-tail presence or other distribution. With an MLM business, you are the promotion. You need to be a self-starter and devote significant time and energy to your distributorship. The trap with MLM is that because it's cheap to get involved, you may not invest the time it will take to be successful. If you spent $100,000 instead of $500, it would have your attention in a different way. In addition, if you go this route, the most important skill you need is sales.

Network marketing systems have been criticized over the years as pyramid and Ponzi schemes. When selecting a program and company to affiliate with, you need to be careful and make sure it's legitimate. My first exposure to MLM was when my aunt Elly sold Amway products in the 1970s. She was as gregarious a person as you'd ever want to meet. I don't think she made much money from the system, which involved selling cleaning products to neighbors and friends, and getting other people to do likewise. The problem with Amway is the problem with most MLM products—they are commodity items like soap, or they are completely useless items like Noni or Goji juice, which not only taste horrible, but you have to convince other people to sell this putrid stuff to their friends.

Not all MLM systems are Amway and weird juices. I started using a new product this year called SendOutCards.com and decided to become a distributor. (To learn more, visit www.sendoutcards. com/58646.)

It's a good example of a system that starts with an excellent, unique product and then offers an optional entrepreneurial business model. With any MLM system you may consider, the most important thing to evaluate is whether the company is most concerned with selling its product or signing up distributors. If their biggest motivation is distributors, that's a warning sign. With SendOutCards, the company puts most of its effort into product development to make its products continually better, more user-friendly, and more sophisticated. It is a "real" business, not a pyramid scheme.

Conclusion:
What Now?

Have I scared you away from your entrepreneurial dreams? If I did, good! That means you were fantasizing and woke up not yet ready to do what it will take to be successful. Take a moment and write down what it is you REALLY want out of life—to drive around the country in an RV for a year, to swim with the dolphins, to move to Idaho and farm potatoes. Be grateful that you aren't going to spend your life savings funding the wrong dreams by buying a franchise and working yourself to the bone.

If I didn't scare you off, that's equally good because you just may be crazy enough to start a business.

A couple of core messages from this book bear repeating as I wrap up.

Above all, you have to understand what is motivating you to consider starting your own business. Nowadays, it is all too common to see people gravitate to business ownership as a default to other possibilities. Because of layoffs, downsizings, and corporate buyouts, hundreds of thousands of people are losing their appetite for the corporate world and traditional jobs. It's natural at least to consider starting your own business as one alternative to getting back on the corporate horse. But for some, all they really need is a vacation, a hobby, or some other mechanism to get their equilibrium back and land another job. Are you sure that's not a possibility for you? It's guaranteed to be easier than starting a business. If it's no longer an option and you must start a business to have the contentment and peace of mind you're after, then more power to you.

Not only must you understand your own mind and the tricks it might be playing on you, but you must also know whether you have the right stuff to be a success in your own business. You have to possess certain core attributes, including the ability to take risk, being excellent at sales, knowing how to think for yourself, and acting as a leader, rather than a follower (even if you are a franchisee "following" a system). You have to learn negotiation skills and you have to be a strange combination of cynic and optimist—cynical enough to know when you are being bamboozled and optimistic enough to overcome the daily obstacles to your business survival.

If you understand yourself and you have (or can develop) what it takes in terms of skills, you need to have the resources to be in it for the long haul. This is a Decathlon to the power of 10. You need cash reserves, support from your family, good health, a team of professionals at your disposal, and a new approach to how you spend your time, so you can have more of it available for your business.

If you decide to pursue investigation of a franchise, you have to be strategic in the way you approach your discussions with the franchisor and other franchisees, realizing that every party has its own agenda and that, in the end, no one is looking out for you but you. You should also seriously consider non-franchise options, of which there are many.

If you are serious about making the transition from executive to entrepreneur, you should hire a professional, certified business coach who has walked in your shoes and who has helped other people like you.

Making this transition can be a solitary and lonely road, but it doesn't have to be. It can also be an invigorating self-discovery journey that leads to tremendous personal empowerment and fulfillment. A coach can help you navigate your way to a positive outcome by helping you shape your dreams into goals that can be methodically achieved. Your family can help you come to the right decision if you involve them deeply in the process.

My success came partly from luck, because I didn't follow my own advice for the first few years of my franchise. Fortunately, my coaches were there to get me on the right path, and my family was always there to support me. I hope that you won't need luck to be successful in your franchise and you can have the outcome you want, as I have—which is pretty nicely described in the end of my son's essay from high school:

It's been roughly four years now since Dad started his business. I now work for him whenever he needs me. I'm no longer ashamed, as he does the absolute best he can, and he's home almost all the time so I can talk to him. He may not make as much money as he used to, he may not command an army of corporate underlings, he may not wear the suit and tie and wield the mighty executive briefcase, but he's a success in my eyes. Money can't buy Happiness, but we've got plenty of both, and most importantly, unlike when I was a child, I now have a father.

Additional Resources for Information on Franchising

Web sites & Newsletters

Entrepreneur.com, the Web site of *Entrepreneur* Magazine, has a ranking called the Franchise 500, with statistics and description of all of them. While the site is a bit of a cheerleader rather than strictly objective, it offers a wealth of information that will save you time when looking for franchises to evaluate.

The Wall Street Journal has excellent content for small businesses and those considering a franchise. You can also search for businesses for sale. http://online.wsj.com/public/page/news-small-business-franchising.html

SmartBrief.com is a newsletter publisher with excellent, free daily briefs on entrepreneurship, franchising, and other related topics. www.smartbrief.com

Inc.com, the Web site of *Inc.* magazine, offers many tutorial articles on franchising. I like their articles because they cover important topics like "10 Common Mistakes of Prospective Franchisees." Many other sites are too busy trying to sell you a franchise to give you information on what to watch out for. www.inc.com

StartupNation.com is a Web site "by entrepreneurs for entrepreneurs." It's very "uncorporate" (which is a good thing). Lots of informative articles and videos and some fun competitions. www.startupnation. com.

Government & Trade Associations

The Small Business Administration has a Web site for older entrepreneurs at www.sba.gov/50plusentrepreneur. The site links to information from the rest of the SBA site, including a self-assessment for entrepreneurs.

The Federal Trade Commission has a site on business opportunities and franchising with numerous downloadable reference documents. http://www.ftc.gov/bcp/franchise/netfran.shtm

The International Franchise Association is the professional association of franchisors. But someone who is interested in franchises can search their database of 1,200 franchises by category and keywords and send inquiries for more information about any that interest you. www. franchise.org.

Consultants

FranChoice is the largest and most respected franchise consultant/broker in the country. I have personally dealt with many of their consultants and found them to be ethical and a great source of information. Just remember they are paid only if you buy a franchise, and you'll be able to use their services within a proper framework. www.franchoice.com

The Entrepreneur's Source. Itself a franchise, E-Source is similar to FranChoice and has knowledgeable consultants. Their Web site, I believe, is somewhat misleading when they state, "We're coaches, not brokers ... we're not trying to sell you anything." Well, yes they actually are. But it's okay. I have met many of their consultants and they have a lot of information to impart that will not cost you anything. www. theesource.com.

Special Offer for Readers

Thank you for reading this Executive-to-Entrepreneur book. If you are considering starting your own business—franchise or otherwise—after your corporate career and would like a free evaluation of your readiness for entrepreneurship, send an e-mail to mitch@e2ecoaching.com with "Evaluation" in the subject line. Briefly describe your current situation, what interests you about entrepreneurship, and how you can be reached. The author will then contact you.

LaVergne, TN USA
16 October 2009
161051LV00002B/23/P